T0372353

Cambridge Elements ≡

Elements in Epistemology
edited by
Stephen Hetherington
University of New South Wales, Sydney

KNOWLEDGE AND GOD

Matthew A. Benton
Seattle Pacific University

Shaftesbury Road, Cambridge CB2 8EA, United Kingdom

One Liberty Plaza, 20th Floor, New York, NY 10006, USA

477 Williamstown Road, Port Melbourne, VIC 3207, Australia

314–321, 3rd Floor, Plot 3, Splendor Forum, Jasola District Centre,
New Delhi – 110025, India

103 Penang Road, #05–06/07, Visioncrest Commercial, Singapore 238467

Cambridge University Press is part of Cambridge University Press & Assessment,
a department of the University of Cambridge.

We share the University's mission to contribute to society through the pursuit of
education, learning and research at the highest international levels of excellence.

www.cambridge.org
Information on this title: www.cambridge.org/9781009533614

DOI: 10.1017/9781009127103

First published 2024

A catalogue record for this publication is available from the British Library.

ISBN 978-1-009-53361-4 Hardback
ISBN 978-1-009-12411-9 Paperback
ISSN 2398-0567 (online)
ISSN 2514-3832 (print)

Knowledge and God

Elements in Epistemology

DOI: 10.1017/9781009127103
First published online: April 2024

Matthew A. Benton
Seattle Pacific University

Author for correspondence: Matthew A. Benton, bentonm@spu.edu

Abstract: This Element examines a main theme in religious epistemology, namely, the possibility of knowledge of God. Most often philosophers consider the rationality or justification of propositional belief about God, particularly beliefs about the existence and nature of God; and they will assess the conditions under which, if there is a God, such propositional beliefs would be knowledge, particularly in light of counterevidence or the availability of religious disagreement. This Element surveys such familiar areas, and then turns toward newer and less-developed terrain: interpersonal epistemology, namely, what it is to know another person. The Element then explores the prospects for understanding what it might take to know God relationally, the contours of which are significant for many theistic traditions.

Keywords: knowledge, God, interpersonal knowledge, epistemology of religion, faith

ISBNs: 9781009533614 (HB), 9781009124119 (PB), 9781009127103 (OC)
ISSNs: 2398-0567 (online), 2514-3832 (print)

Contents

1 Preliminaries

Philosophers working in epistemology typically seek to understand the nature of propositional knowledge. Where propositions are the contents of one's beliefs about reality, such propositions are true just in case they represent part of how the world in fact is, and false when they represent how the world is not. Epistemologists typically focus on how we can form (and sustain) beliefs that are ensured to be, or at least more likely to be, true; and when they are true, epistemologists examine the conditions under which such beliefs would be knowledge. One classic approach is to assess the evidence or arguments supporting one's beliefs: how sensory perception, one's reasoning processes, one's reliance on memory or on others' testimony, makes one's beliefs more reliable, even if fallible.

Epistemologists also wonder about *how much* we can know, and about which domains. Knowledge about the empirical world is perhaps one thing. But what about our beliefs in the areas of long past history, or mathematics, or morality, or politics? Or religion? A common view is that for many of these domains, it is much harder, and perhaps nearly impossible, to acquire knowledge. When considering the God of the monotheistic traditions, gaining *knowledge* about the existence and (if there is such a being) the attributes of God is often assumed to be out of reach. Philosophical examination of the possibility of such knowledge often focuses on arguments for and against the existence of God. The most prominent arguments for theism tend to be ontological arguments, such as those descending from Anselm, as well as cosmological arguments, teleological or (recently) fine-tuning arguments, moral arguments, and so on. The most prominent arguments against theism are from the problem of evil and suffering, or from divine hiddenness. These arguments are sophisticated and often quite technical, and philosophers disagree over which arguments are strongest. As such they also disagree over what, if anything, people should believe as a result. Thus, it is most often felt that the matter of whether there is a God is not demonstratively clear one way or the other.[1] Thus, philosophers (and many others) settle for talk of religious *beliefs* about the existence or nature of God, and similarly for atheistic belief: The common cultural question tends to be whether one believes that there is a God, not whether one *knows* that there is, or is not, a God. As such, the typical questions turn to what makes for justified or responsibly held theistic (or atheistic) beliefs, or under what conditions one might, with agnostics, withhold belief on the matter.

---

[1] And then such entrenched disagreement is sometimes invoked against the plausibility of theism. For recent work on the epistemology of religious disagreement, see De Cruz (2019), Pittard (2020), and the essays in Benton and Kvanvig (2021).

This section considers a brief retrospective of how these issues are often framed, beginning with three influential parables from Antony Flew, R. M. Hare, and Basil Mitchell.[2] These parables orient us to three different views of religious epistemology, two of which dominated the themes of discussion for the last century, but one of which remains to be carefully developed; the sections of this Element aim to provide an account of this neglected theme. Looking ahead, Section 2 considers the nature of propositional knowledge in general, and how plausibly someone might gain knowledge that God exists, even given concerns about defeat and disagreement. Section 3 will draw on important recent work in epistemology concerning objectual or qualitative knowledge, practical knowledge, and interpersonal knowledge, in an attempt to motivate a broader approach to epistemology which moves beyond the focus on propositional knowledge. While such advances are independently motivated, we shall, in section 4, propose significant applications of them in religious epistemology, including one that several theistic traditions already recognize. Finally, Section 5 articulates an account of theistic faith in terms of the lessons learned from earlier sections.

1.1 Three Parables

Antony Flew adapted an anecdote from John Wisdom (1945) in order to lodge a combined epistemic and linguistic criticism concerning religious belief:

> Once upon a time two explorers came upon a clearing in the jungle. In the clearing were growing many flowers and many weeds. One explorer says, "some gardener must tend this plot." The other disagrees, "there is no gardener." So they pitch their tents and set a watch. No gardener is ever seen. "But perhaps he is an invisible gardener." So they set up a barbed-wire fence. They electrify it. They patrol with bloodhounds. . . . But no shrieks ever suggest that some intruder has received a shock. No movements of the wire ever betray an invisible climber. The bloodhounds never give cry. Yet still the Believer is not convinced. "But there is a gardener, invisible, intangible, insensible to electric shocks, a gardener who has no scent and makes no sound, a gardener who comes secretly to look after the garden which he loves." At last the Sceptic despairs, "But what remains of your original assertion? Just how does what you call an invisible, intangible, eternally elusive gardener differ from an imaginary gardener or even from no gardener at all?"

---

[2] From a symposium on Theology and Falsification, published in a now-defunct Oxford journal *University*, 1950–51, repr. in Flew, Hare, and Mitchell (1955) and in many later philosophy of religion anthologies.

Flew sums up his concern by noting that "[a] fine brash hypothesis may thus be killed by inches, the death by a thousand qualifications" (Flew, Hare, and Mitchell 1955, 96–97). Flew's own discussion is unfortunately couched in the then prevailing orthodoxy of logical positivism (particularly given its expression, in Oxford, by Ayer 1936[3]): Flew invokes a falsification principle in order to focus on the *meaning* of the one explorer's assertion that a gardener must tend the plot. For Flew, the meaning of the explorer's assertion is given by the evidential conditions under which they could verify or falsify its truth, as opposed to the conditions under which it would be true. Flew explains that if we are in doubt about what someone meant by their assertive utterance, we can

> attempt to find what he would regard as counting against, or as being incompatible with, its truth. For if the utterance is indeed an assertion, it will necessarily be equivalent to a denial of the negation of that assertion. And anything which would count against the assertion, or which would induce the speaker to withdraw it and to admit that it had been mistaken, must be part of (or the whole of) the meaning of the negation of that assertion. (Flew, Hare, and Mitchell 1955, 98)

Thus, Flew seems to insist along with Ayer that such religious assertions are "meaningless." But with the benefit of later developments in philosophy of language, we can see that the epistemological issues are distinct from the semantic issues: evidence which would count against my belief that p, expressed by my asserting "p," isn't part of the *meaning* of my assertion. Suppose I assert "All emeralds are green," and a budding gemologist counters this by pointing out (falsely) that some emeralds have been found which are red. Her testimony might be treated as evidence against my claim, and might lead me to retreat to "Oh, well that's what I had learned"; or it might be rebuffed if I knew this rumor to be wrong. But my epistemic position (or dialectical ability) has no bearing on what the initial claim *meant*. A declarative utterance's meaning is connected to its truth conditions, not its verification or falsification conditions. Difficulty (or ease) in empirically confirming (or disconfirming) some declarative claim doesn't change its meaning: It will be true or false depending on how the world is, quite apart from whether we are well-positioned to discern how the world is. "The number of planets in the Milky Way galaxy is even" means what it does apart from whether any of us could ever verify it.

---

[3] Philosophical theologians had to reckon with the dominance of such positivism, particularly around Oxford; see especially Mitchell (1958). Cf. the introduction to Dole and Chignell (2005) for philosophical reception of the next half century; and Knight (2013) for two major twentieth century theological responses to the positivism of Ayer, Flew (incl. Flew 1966), and others.

We need not accept Flew's semantic theory in order to acknowledge the important epistemological issue raised by the parable: It can seem increasingly irrational to accept a hypothesis when the evidence one would expect to find for it goes lacking. Flew's believing explorer is insufficiently responsive to new evidence which fails to confirm his hypothesis that some gardener (still) tends the plot, and this seems to be mounting evidence *against* his (initial) hypothesis. Continuing to qualify the hypothesis in response looks like a desperate attempt to save it, rather than reduce one's confidence in it. And Flew's deeper concern is that a theist, much like his gardener-believing explorer, is insufficiently responsive to the evidence, particularly when significant counterevidence emerges, such as the evidence of evil and suffering which seem to tell against the Christian theist's belief that there is a God of love.[4]

R. M. Hare's response invoked his own parable, of a lunatic student who thinks all the university faculty are out to get him:

> A certain lunatic is convinced that all dons [university professors] want to murder him. His friends introduce him to all the mildest and most respectable dons that they can find, and after each of them has retired, they say, "You see, he doesn't really want to murder you; he spoke to you in a most cordial manner; surely you are convinced now?" But the lunatic replies, "Yes, but that was only his diabolical cunning; he's really plotting against me the whole time, like the rest of them; I know it I tell you." However many kindly dons are produced, the reaction is still the same. (Flew, Hare, and Mitchell 1955, 99–100)

Hare's case is much like Flew's gardener-believing explorer, in that they both seem to be improperly responsive to evidence, though for the lunatic student, the failure is plausibly one of not responding to counterevidence against his belief (rather than a failure to appreciate the ongoing lack of evidence for it). For "there is no behaviour of dons that can be enacted which he will accept as counting against his theory" (1955, 100).

---

[4] "...it often seems to people who are not religious as if there was no conceivable event or series of events the occurrence of which would be admitted by sophisticated religious people to be a sufficient reason for conceding 'there wasn't a God after all' or 'God does not really love us then.' Someone tells us that God loves us as a father loves his children. We are reassured. But then we see a child dying of inoperable cancer of the throat. His earthly father is driven frantic in his efforts to help, but his Heavenly Father reveals no obvious sign of concern. Some qualification is made—God's love is 'not a merely human love' or it is 'an inscrutable love', perhaps—and we realize that such sufferings are quite compatible with the truth of the assertion that 'God loves us as a father (but, of course, ...)'. We are reassured again. But then perhaps we ask: what is this assurance of God's (appropriately qualified) love worth, what is this apparent guarantee really a guarantee against? Just what would have to happen not merely (morally and wrongly) to tempt but also (logically and rightly) to entitle us to say 'God does not love us' or even 'God does not exist'?" (Flew, Hare, and Mitchell 1955, 98–99).

Hare argues against Flew's approach to dismissing the believer's claim as meaningless. Though Hare seems to accept Flew's use of the semantic theory, he hopes to show that the function of certain beliefs (or belief-like commitments) reveals their roles in one's motivation and reasoning. For Hare, the lunatic student has a *blik*:

> Let us call that in which we differ from this lunatic, our respective *bliks*. He has an insane *blik* about dons; we have a sane one. It is important to realize that we have a sane one, not no *blik* at all; for there must be two sides to any argument – if he has a wrong *blik*, then those who are right about dons must have a right one. (1955, 100)[5]

Hare insists that such *bliks* are not like standard beliefs which are, or should be, responsive to evidence; rather, they are presupposed in order for us to interpret what the evidence supports, perhaps even nonrational. The mistake of Flew's position, Hare suggests, "is to regard this kind of talk as some sort of *explanation*, as scientists are accustomed to use the word ... as Hume saw, without a *blik* there can be no explanation; for it is by our *bliks* that we decide what is and what is not an explanation" (1955, 101). Thus, for Hare, the student's and the theist's *bliks* arguably function like hinge propositions: They frame what evidence is, and how it supports hypotheses (much like what formal epistemologists call a prior probability function). As Wittgenstein earlier (circa 1950–51) put it, "the *questions* that we raise and our *doubts* depend upon the fact that some propositions are exempt from doubt, are as it were like hinges on which those turn" (Wittgenstein 1969, §341; cf. Pritchard 2000, 2012).

So Flew's and Hare's parables each characterize the theist as not responsive to evidence against their theistic commitments, although each in somewhat different ways. Flew's explorer continued to qualify his belief, thinning it out so as to change what evidence should be expected given it; whereas Hare's student's *blik* about dons remained intact, and it was so deeply embedded in the student's psyche that it served to constrain how they interpreted all new evidence. Hare also noted a further difference, namely, that the explorers are somewhat detached, not much minding about which of their hypotheses is true, whereas the student cares greatly about his, given the practical stakes for him about it (Flew, Hare, and Mitchell 1955, 103).

Basil Mitchell, writing in reply to both Flew and Hare, offers his own parable which borrows elements from each of their examples. Mitchell responds in

---

[5] Note how paradoxical Hare's line is, accepting Flew's semantic theory that the student's *blik* (if verbalized) "asserts nothing," but also assessing that *blik* as "wrong," since "those who are right about dons must have a right" *blik*. But if we are right about dons, that'd be because it's *true* that they are not out to murder, in which case its assertion cannot be meaningless.

partial agreement with Flew, namely, that theological utterances ought to count as assertions, and he also agrees about how theists should respond to the evidence: Mitchell acknowledges that the theist should treat some evidence, particularly facts about suffering, as counting against their beliefs.[6] He likewise sides with Hare in thinking that the theist's interests are not those of a detached observer, but of faithful commitment to trusting God. Thus, Mitchell insists that the theist's view, including the nature of their initial experience and evidence, should be reconceived in interpersonal terms. Mitchell illustrates this through his own parable of the Partisan and the Stranger:

> In time of war in an occupied country, a member of the resistance meets one night a stranger who deeply impresses him. They spend that night together in conversation. The Stranger tells the partisan that he himself is on the side of the resistance – indeed that he is in command of it, and urges the partisan to have faith in him no matter what happens. The partisan is utterly convinced at that meeting of the Stranger's sincerity and constancy and undertakes to trust him.
>
> They never meet in conditions of intimacy again. But sometimes the Stranger is seen helping members of the resistance, and the partisan is grateful and says to his friends, "He is on our side."
>
> Sometimes he is seen in the uniform of the police handing over patriots to the occupying power. On these occasions his friends murmur against him; but the partisan still says, "He is on our side." He still believes that, in spite of appearances, the Stranger did not deceive him. Sometimes he asks the Stranger for help and receives it. He is then thankful. Sometimes he asks and does not receive it. Then he says, "the Stranger knows best." Sometimes his friends, in exasperation, say, "Well, what *would* he have to do for you to admit that you were wrong and that he is not on our side?" But the partisan refuses to answer. He will not consent to put the Stranger to the test. . . .
>
> The partisan of the parable does not allow anything to count decisively against the proposition "the Stranger is on our side." This is because he has committed himself to trust the Stranger. But he of course recognizes that the Stranger's ambiguous behavior *does* count against what he believes about him. It is precisely this situation which constitutes the trial of his faith.
>
> When the partisan asks for help and doesn't get it, what can he do? He can (*a*) conclude that the stranger is not on our side; or (*b*) maintain that he is on our side, but that he has reasons for withholding help.
>
> The first he will refuse to do. How long can he uphold the second position without its becoming just silly?
>
> I don't think one can say in advance. It will depend on the nature of the impression created by the Stranger in the first place. (Flew, Hare, and Mitchell 1955, 103–104)

---

[6] For clarity on the epistemological details of this view, in light of much recent literature on the skeptical theist response to the problem of evil, see Benton, Hawthorne, and Isaacs (2016).

Mitchell explains that the partisan's belief that the stranger is on their side is different from the *bliks* from Hare's parable, and in multiple ways. First, the partisan does feel the ongoing force of the evidence against his belief, and trust, in the stranger; whereas the student does not admit that anything counts against his *blik*. Second, the partisan has a reason for his belief in the stranger, owing to their encounter and his understanding of the stranger's character; whereas the student has no reason for their *blik* about dons. Third, Mitchell likewise thinks of the partisan's belief as an *explanation*, for "it explains and makes sense of the stranger's behavior." Moreover, Mitchell argues against Flew (and Hare) that the partisan's assertion of his belief in the stranger, much like a theist's that "God loves us," does indeed count as meaningful and an assertion (1955, 105).

1.2 Two Lessons

One significant lesson of these parables is that philosophers should examine what sorts of evidence or arguments contribute to a belief about God being rational or being knowledge, while being wary of how ancillary matters (such as whatever semantic theory is currently en vogue) might lead one astray.[7]

A second lesson, for our purposes, involves a crucial aspect of Mitchell's parable, and one which is also the least often discussed: It involves two people meeting and relating to each other, wherein the personal encounter between them enables the partisan to assess and understand the stranger's character. The partisan learns of the stranger's existence in a way which supports placing trust in him. The initial experience was interpersonal, of the sort which happens when one begins to know someone else personally, in relationship.[8] A natural way of understanding the partisan's scenario is comparable to many of our other personal interactions: what one person learns about the other in many such encounters is sufficiently rich as to provide rational support in the face of much doubt. If so, the epistemologist would like to have a fuller account of such knowledge, how it is acquired and sustained, and why it might matter. Given the importance of our human relationships and of social cognition,

---

[7] Another example of this is medieval mystics' pessimism in the epistemology of testimony, which flows from their emotionist semantics and strong readings of *de re* content: see Fraser (2018).

[8] The account to be developed here thus aims to recover scattered interpersonal themes from the first half of the twentieth century, e.g., in C. C. J. Webb (1911 and 1920); William James (1912); John Cook Wilson (1926a); Norman Kemp Smith (1931), who called for an "altered theory of knowledge"; Martin Buber (1937); John Baillie (1939); a young John Rawls (1941; unpublished until 2009); C. S. Lewis (1955 and 1959); and H. H. Price (1965), among others.

we might well hope to make progress on understanding the details of an inter-personal epistemology more generally, unseating the dominant framework of propositional belief.[9] A philosopher of religion focusing on theism has a particular interest in how it might work should there be a God to whom humans might be related in structurally similar ways.

The most prominent theistic voices in religious epistemology of the last generation focused primarily on religious *belief*, and sometimes on *propositional* knowledge about God, but rarely examined what it might be to know God in some relational sense. William Alston, in his important book *Perceiving God*, acknowledges that his central thesis throughout concerns only the epistemic justification, rationality, and reliability of (propositional) belief about God, and says almost nothing about propositional knowledge.[10] Similarly Richard Swinburne defends theism as rational given a probabilistic framework for belief, but has little to say about propositional knowledge (Swinburne 2005, 63–65; cf. 2001, Chap. 8). Alvin Plantinga, in *Warranted Christian Belief* (2000), is focused primarily on a notion of warranted belief given his proper function-alist account of justification (developed more fully in Plantinga 1993), which he connects to the possibility of propositional knowledge.[11] Where Plantinga explicitly invokes such knowledge as part of his "Extended Aquinas/Calvin model" of what faith involves, he rarely appeals to knowing God in any personal or relational sense.[12] To his credit, Nicholas Wolterstorff gestured briefly, in early writings, at the connection between knowing and having faith in God,[13] but he says little else until very recent work (Wolterstorff 2016, 2021).

This not a criticism of these philosophers, for any recent work in epistemology of religion owes much to their pioneering work. In particular, arguments by Alston, Swinburne, Plantinga, Wolterstorff, and others did much to dissolve several philosophical objections to theistic belief according to which such belief is subpar by being irrational or unreasonable because it was thought to

---

[9] Note that Judaism arguably lacks the recent emphasis on belief: cf. Lebens (2013, 2023).

[10] Except for two pages, Alston (1991, 284–285).

[11] Plantinga regards warrant as whatever property turns true belief into knowledge. Yet understood this way, one could never have warranted false beliefs, and it is less clear how to evaluate true but unwarranted beliefs about God (he argues that "if Christian belief is true, then it is also warranted" (Plantinga 2000, xii), and that "the question whether theistic belief has *warrant* is not, after all, independent of the question whether theistic belief is *true*," 191).

[12] Though see Plantinga (2000, 256–58, incl. fn. 30, and Ch. 9) on religious affections.

[13] "To have faith in God is to know him; to know God is to have faith in him" (Wolterstorff, Introduction to Plantinga and Wolterstorff 1983, 15); and "Interpretation of a person's discourse occurs, and can only occur, in the context of knowledge of that person. . . . So too for God: to interpret God's discourse more reliably, we must come to know God better" (Wolterstorff 1995, 239).

be insufficiently supported by argument or (certain sorts of) evidence.[14] We only note then that their arguments were centered on responding to skeptical concerns over whether and how one can hold rational or justified beliefs about God.[15]

Recent mainstream epistemology has largely turned away from "classical" (Cartesian) foundationalist and internalist views of knowledge which were more widely accepted during that earlier period, and which drove the common objections to theistic belief. Narrow or "classical" foundationalism held that all knowledge we might have comes from a limited range of sources of (or kinds of) evidence, such as through sensory perception, memory, reasoning, or some combination thereof. Some forms of internalism often complemented such a foundationalist picture, according to which the evidence on which one's beliefs are based must, if such beliefs are to be knowledge, be immediately accessible or available to one.

Yet such accounts struggled to explain how it is that we commonly acquire knowledge from another person's testimony, an especially pressing problem given how much of what we know is socially dependent on others' knowledge. Such views likewise seem unable to explain how we can know a great deal about other people, like those we interact with daily. John Greco nicely summarizes these inadequacies: such foundationalisms and internalisms try

> to explain all of our knowledge in terms of too few sources of knowledge, too limited a variety of evidence. One place this becomes evident is regarding our *knowledge of persons*. How is it that we know what other persons are thinking or feeling, or that they have minds at all? If we have a limited conception of the sources of knowledge, it will be very hard to say. (Greco 2017, 10; italics mine)

As Greco notes, mainstream epistemology has largely moved beyond this outdated approach to knowledge, turning more toward broadly externalist approaches to knowledge, such as causal, or reliabilist, or proper functionalist, or virtue epistemology theories, or even "knowledge-first" approaches to epistemology which regard knowledge as the fundamental and unanalyzable notion in terms of which epistemic theorizing is to be done.[16] Contemporary

---

[14] See especially Plantinga (1967); Swinburne (2004 (1st ed., 1979)); Alston (1982); Plantinga and Wolterstorff (1983) (Alston, "Christian Experience and Christian Belief," especially 103–110; Plantinga, "Reason and Belief in God," at 20–39; and Wolterstorff, "Can Belief in God Be Rational If It Has No Foundations?," sects. 3–7); and Plantinga (2000, Ch. 3). See Moon (2016) and McNabb (2019) for apt overviews of "Reformed" epistemology.

[15] See Dunaway and Hawthorne (2017) on skepticism about theism.

[16] See especially Goldman (1967 and 1986) for causal and reliabilist views; Plantinga (1993) and Bergmann (2006) for proper-functionalist accounts; Sosa (2007) and Greco (2010) for virtue epistemology; Williamson (2000) for knowledge-first epistemology. Most such externalist

theorizing also draws on related advances in the cognitive sciences, which have discovered that human cognition depends on "a rich variety of integrated modules or faculties, each with its own job to do in different domains of knowledge" (Greco 2017, 10).

Importantly for our focus, Greco situates the present state of play thus: "Religious epistemology and the epistemology of theology have followed suit, by rejecting outdated models of our knowledge of God," a movement borne out by much recent work.[17] Greco continues:

> Most prominently, both now challenge the idea that our knowledge of God must be by means of 'proofs' or 'demonstrations', as if knowledge of God were akin to knowledge of mathematical theorems. On the contrary, contemporary religious epistemology takes seriously the idea that our knowledge of God is a kind of knowledge of persons. But in general, our knowledge of persons is by means of our interpersonal experience of them, as well as by means of what they reveal about themselves with their own words and actions. Religious epistemology is nowadays interested in pursuing analogous models of our knowledge of a personal God. (Greco 2017, 10–11)

Thus in this Element we shall be less preoccupied with arguing against skepticism or charges of irrationality, and shall aim to make progress on what other sorts of knowledge of God one might have, with a focus on what _interpersonal_ knowledge of God might involve. The overall approach centers the notion(s) of knowledge in order to reveal the many dimensions of cognition which we already recognize in human affairs, and to assess how plausibly they might apply to us with respect to God, if there is a God. This is highly relevant given that the lived experience of many religious believers includes a nuanced understanding of their religious experiences and the practices through which they encounter God.[18]

In Section 2 we shall survey some views about propositional knowledge in general, and the possibility of propositional knowledge about God, if there is

---

views are coupled with a version of foundationalism (understood merely as the view that there are some beliefs, or sources of them, which are properly basic and not derived from other sources); yet such views are more permissive about those sources than the broadly classical foundationalism dominant even up through the mid-twentieth century. For discussion of "classical" versus more plausible foundationalisms, see Plantinga (2000, 82–99), and Bergmann (2017).

[17] Note, e.g., that the essays in Benton, Hawthorne, and Rabinowitz (2018), or Ellis (2018), or recent articles like Griffioen (2022), contain very little mention of foundationalism or internalism.

[18] "Knowing God involves training, and it involves interpretation ... as people acquire the knowledge and the practices through which they come to know that God, the most intimate aspects of the way they experience their everyday world change. ...They have different evidence for what is true" (Luhrmann 2012, 226; cf. 317–321. See especially Luhrmann 2020 for more).

indeed a God. (If there is no God, the relevant question concerns the possibility of the atheist's knowledge: propositional knowledge that no God exists.) We briefly consider the common features that any such knowledge would have to involve, whether it be derived from natural theology arguments, from others' testimony about what they know, from divinely revealed sacred texts, or from a religious experience of God.

In Section 3 we turn to several other sorts of knowledge that might be available, particularly *objectual* knowledge, *practical* knowledge (knowledge-how), and *interpersonal* knowledge. We discuss the relationship between these types of knowledge and propositional knowledge, and then examine Eleonore Stump's notion of "Franciscan knowledge" of God (Stump 2010, 2017).[19] Drawing on other work, I then develop a view of what having interpersonal knowledge of God would plausibly involve (Benton 2017, 2018a). In Section 4 we explore how people might have these different sorts of knowledge of God, including how they might come apart from each other. Section 5 concludes by exploring an account of what theistic faith is given the epistemic resources we have developed.

2 Propositional Knowledge and Its Limits

2.1 Knowledge of Facts

Most contemporary philosophers, in line with a broadly common sense view, accept that we know a lot about the world. Epistemologists virtually all agree that such propositional knowledge is knowledge of facts. We believe propositions about the world, where to believe involves (at least) a kind of mental commitment to the world being that way, where such a belief will inform one's other beliefs and guide one's actions. A constitutive feature of belief is that it aims at the truth, and thus a belief is in one important sense better – indeed, best – if it is true. Yet some beliefs are, or count as, or amount to, knowledge. A main difference between such knowledge and mere belief is that beliefs can be false, whereas knowledge cannot: We can only have propositional knowledge of truths, and thus epistemologists sometimes say that knowledge is "factive." When we claim propositional knowledge, whether for ourselves or others, we seem to be making two claims at once: We're claiming something about the way somebody is (that they hold a belief), and also something about the way the world is (that their belief is true). Much epistemological theorizing takes

---

[19] Related work which I won't be able to engage with includes Green (2015) and Cockayne (2020).

this as a point of departure and asks: What is the difference between knowing a proposition p, and believing that p when p is true?

The answer must, it seems, involve a normative notion which was earlier labeled "justification" (or sometimes "warrant" or "entitlement"), about which internalists and externalists offered different accounts. Such rivals aimed to explain why an accidentally true belief, such as when one's belief is based on evidence that luckily just happens to point to the truth, still seems not to count as knowledge. In the decades after Gettier 1963, externalist epistemologists appealed to belief-forming (or belief-sustaining) processes that are reliable or properly functioning in their environment, or are modally sensitive or modally safe, or which exhibit competence (among others). Although sometimes such processes could also give one "evidence" or "reasons" of the sort which internalists often require, these philosophers argue that such internal states are not needed: So long as these external conditions hold such that one formed one's belief in a sufficiently reliable (or sensitive, or safe, etc.) manner, one's true belief would also be knowledge.[20] To illustrate, on a *proper functionalist* account of sensory perception, if an agent believes that p as a result of her perceptual faculties (such as vision), which are properly functioning in the sort of environment for which her visual sensory faculty was designed, and p is true, she thereby knows that p. Or, on a *safety* theory, knowledge requires, roughly, that one could not easily have been wrong in a similar case. So if our agent forms her belief on the basis of vision (used in a suitable environment to see moderate size objects, at a close distance, under decent lighting conditions, etc.), and using her vision in such circumstances is a belief-forming method by which she would not easily have formed a false belief that p, then she knows that p.[21] Importantly, one need not also be aware of such conditions, for such externalists deny that the agent must also verify or have reason to believe that such appropriate conditions hold: to require that would be to impose an implausible further condition on knowledge. In addition, externalists typically deny that when one knows, one will always be in a position to know that, or how, one knows.

In line with most contemporary epistemologists, I shall assume a broadly externalist view of the normative conditions needed for propositional knowledge. For simplicity's sake I shall typically call them "safe" methods, without thereby supposing that a safety theory of knowledge must be correct. And I shall

---

[20] See Srinivasan (2020) for an important recent defense of externalism.

[21] More specifically, but still roughly, a belief b held by a subject S is safe just in case in all "nearby" worlds w, or worlds that could easily have obtained, if S has the belief b in w, then S's belief b is true in w. See especially Sosa (1999) and Williamson (2000, Ch. 7), for more detailed discussions.

assume that such structural features likewise apply to our propositional knowledge, if any, about God. Given that knowledge is factive, one cannot know that God exists, or that God is a certain way, if those facts do not obtain. Thus, to simplify our discussion I shall assume that a God exists much like that common to the major monotheistic traditions of Judaism, Christianity, and Islam.[22] So I will not be arguing here that God exists,[23] but rather arguing that if God exists and the externalist conditions are right, then humans can sometimes come to have propositional knowledge (and even other sorts of knowledge, discussed in later sections) of God. Thus, if God exists, theists will have many true beliefs, and they would be united as theists in the correctness of their belief that a God exists. Of course, some of these theists' further beliefs about God might be, or fail to be, knowledge, depending on how reliable or safe (etc.) their belief-forming (or -sustaining) methods are, though I shall not be taking a stand on in what, exactly, those conditions consist.[24] On the other hand, if there is no God, then no one has propositional knowledge of God, and indeed, if atheism is true, then it might be quite easy for the atheist to have knowledge of it, or at least of propositions which entail it. For example, after witnessing a brutal case of moral evil, someone might come to know that a morally praiseworthy being would have stopped it if they could have; and infer from this that no morally perfect and omnipotent being exists (see Benton, Hawthorne, and Isaacs (2016), 25–27).[25]

Suppose then that there is a God, and a person believes this. Their belief is true, but whether it counts as knowledge depends on how they arrived at that belief, that is, on the method by which they formed the belief. If their method involves examining several (deductive) natural theology arguments for theism, and such arguments are valid and also have true premises which they also believe, then this method seems suitably safe or reliable, for deduction using a sound argument is a safe method of forming true beliefs. Or suppose that some of the arguments examined are not deductive but probabilistic, or perhaps

---

[22] I mean this very loosely: That God exists is the hypothesis that an extremely knowledgeable, extremely powerful, extremely benevolent being, who created the universe, exists.

[23] For such arguments, see, e.g., Swinburne (2004) or Oppy (2006).

[24] For the record, I am sympathetic to Williamson's (2000) knowledge-first epistemology, which deploys a safety-theoretic account to illuminate the modal features of propositional knowledge without thereby using it to analyze or define knowledge. I am also sympathetic to his E = K thesis, on which one's evidence is all and only one's (propositional) knowledge. For some applications of this view in religious epistemology, see Benton, Hawthorne, and Isaacs (2016, especially §12); Anderson (2018, 24–27); and Dietz and Hawthorne (2023).

[25] However, this would be complicated if knowledge is susceptible to pragmatic encroachment (which I haven't space to consider here); if so, then arguably it would be much harder for an atheist to know atheism (if true) than for the theist to know theism (if theism is true): see Benton (2018b) for a lengthy discussion.

involve inference to the best explanation, such as recently refined arguments from the fine-tuning of the cosmos.[26] If the arguments examined are cogent, with a true conclusion, and they come to believe theism on this basis, it seems possible for them to have gained knowledge of the conclusion. In this case, it similarly seems like a safe method, one by which not easily would one have formed a false belief in a similar case by using the same method: for by using it they formed a true belief, and in nearby worlds in which they use such deductive or inductive methods, they would not yield false beliefs.[27]

Suppose instead though that our believer's method of belief formation involved nothing as strong as evaluating natural theology arguments, but rather is based on believing the *testimony* of someone else that there is a God. Views on the epistemology of testimony diverge over several details, so let's consider more than one account. On a *reductionist* account of the epistemology of testimony, testimony is not a distinctive source of knowledge on a par with other sources such as sense perception or reason. Because of this, many philosophers insist that to come to know by trusting a speaker whose testimony claims that p, one cannot simply go on a default trust of their say-so and thereby come to know that p; one must have some additional, often inductive grounds, for trusting the speaker, or trusting their testimony (on this matter at least), as being reliable. Or perhaps the hearer must at least utilize some (perhaps subconscious) monitoring of their manner so as to pick up on subtle clues that they might be lying or less than fully confident of what they testify to. Thus such reductionists argue that acquiring knowledge from another's testimony requires deploying some of the resources of perception or inductive reasoning (or some combination of them), because they think of testimony as being reducible to those other basic sources of justification, and it is those other sources which give one the needed positive reasons for relying on their testimony on that occasion.[28] On this view, a hearer could come to know from another's testimony that God exists only if their method of believing their testimony is suitably safe, where the hearer's method includes utilizing their more basic sources of justification so as to give

---

[26] See Hawthorne and Isaacs (2018).

[27] This isn't trivial, secured by assuming that God's existence is a necessary truth (and so true at all worlds). It's rather because using a safe method with true inputs is liable to yield (only) true outputs: Thus, deductive reasoning in mathematics gives one knowledge not because mathematical truths are necessary truths but because the methods of deriving them are safe. Cf. Dunaway and Hawthorne (2017, 291): "If one forms mathematical beliefs about large sums by random guessing, and one happens to guess the sum of 85 and 24 correctly, there is no way for the belief that $85 + 24 = 109$ to be false in nearby worlds. But by virtue of arriving at one's beliefs in sums by mere guessing, one will form similar (though not strictly identical) false beliefs in nearby worlds. It is plausible that this kind of risk of error is incompatible with knowing the relevant sums."

[28] See Fricker (1995) and Lackey (2008) for more.

one further positive reasons for trusting the testimony. By contrast, *nonreductionists* about testimony do not require such further positive reasons, for they typically regard testimony itself as a basic source of justification, alongside the widely accepted sources of sense perception and reason. Simplifying considerably, nonreductionists tend to make the possibility of knowledge from testimony less intellectually demanding, which allows us to deem even very young children as commonly gaining knowledge from testimony, whereas reductionists make knowledge from testimony a bit more demanding, thereby ensuring that meeting its standards is less common yet not so easy that even the gullible and irresponsible can come to know all manner of things.

Since the reductionist's view is more demanding, let's consider an example using it: A subject receives testimony that God exists from someone else who (let's suppose) knows this. Perhaps they hear this from them on many occasions, while also regarding them as trustworthy and honest on many other matters as well: the hearer knows plenty about this theist, observes them to be a careful thinker about many other issues, is duly responsive to evidence and arguments, evincing humility when they occasionally get other matters wrong and revise their beliefs accordingly. Perhaps they even observe moral or spiritual fruits of their religious convictions in this believer's life. However we articulate what sorts of positive reasons would be needed in such a case, it seems like some cases of testimony about the truth of theism could evince them, and that a hearer could have such reasons in support in order to rationally believe the theist's testimony, thereby coming to know. (That is a case of interpersonal communication between two people; but one might argue, in line with many theistic traditions, that their tradition's scripture or sacred texts are, or can serve as a vehicle for, divine testimony to us. If so, it might even be possible for such texts to serve as a reliable or safe testimonial source which God uses to speak to us. Arguing that one must first have positive reasons for trusting such sources, and what exactly those positive reasons might be and whether we could appreciate them as such, is beyond the scope of our discussion here.[29])

Finally, maybe our theist believes not on the basis of arguments for God's existence, nor on the basis of testimony from a theist who knows it. Instead they believe God exists because they've had a vivid, quasi-perceptual experience which they took to be of God, and on that basis believe there is such a divine being. If God indeed provided this religious experience and it was in part God that they encountered through their experience, it is quite unclear why this couldn't be a safe method. In particular, if God intends to reveal God's self by providing someone with such an experience, with the aim of getting them

---

[29] But see Plantinga (2000, Ch. 12), or Wolterstorff (1995, Ch. 16).

to believe certain propositions about God (including that God exists), believing that such experiences are indeed of God ought to be safe in something like the way most of our mundane sensory experiences reliably lead to true perceptual beliefs (see Alston 1991). Or at least, such a method could be safe if it is not also a product of cognitive processes involving illusory experiences. (See Section 2.2 for more on defeat and doubt.)

A reflective person, of course, might, upon considering such an experience and what it means, decide after reflection they have no better explanation for their having such an experience than that God provided them such an experience. If so, the reflective believer might be combining two safe methods: the religious experience and their own abductive argument with the experience featuring as a premise. (Many people have been converted to their religious commitments precisely by such experiences, so it seems implausible that all such experiences can be chalked up to such persons unconsciously desiring to have such experiences, or that they generate such experiences, perhaps by unconscious mechanisms of wish-fulfillment, to confirm their already held beliefs.[30] For *ex hypothesi*, those who convert on the basis of such religious experiences did not previously hold the relevant religious beliefs.)

These sketches are not meant to imply that such safe belief-forming methods are easy to come by. It might be that in some circumstances they are unavailable because, for example, the sorts of theistic arguments one is shown are poorly formulated and thus subtly invalid; or, to take another example, perhaps the person whose testimony one hears is such that they themselves formed their own theistic beliefs in unsafe, substandard ways. Common as those may be, such methods are not all that similar to the safe methods one might in fact use.

Another clarification is worth making: While I have argued that it is quite possible for a theist to have acquired propositional knowledge that God exists through safe or otherwise suitably reliable methods, it seems plausible that many, even most, religious believers are not nearly as conscientious in their beliefs as the these cases make out, at least when they initially form their beliefs. Thus, any reflection on the reasons or arguments for which they might believe might only surface later, as they decide whether to maintain such beliefs. Recall though that on an externalist view of knowledge, one does not need to take a stance on whether, or how, one's belief was formed in a reliable or safe manner. As such, the unreflective believer might in some cases have knowledge nevertheless. But for the reflective believer, it is unlikely that in coming to their theistic beliefs they would use only one of the already-mentioned methods. More likely, they would use several of the aforementioned methods in tandem:

---

[30] Cf. Allison (2022).

the recipients of testimony from others about God's existence and attributes, given that most theists are parts of social communities of theists who learn from each other and worship together, are also likely to have acquired some knowledge through reading sacred texts which purport to offer a chain of testimony which, suitably interpreted, can provide knowledge about God. In some cases they might also receive vivid experiences of God which serve to reinforce or confirm their beliefs. When these overlapping methods occur, their overall methods of sustaining their earlier beliefs plausibly must be evaluated as a whole, such that their potential safety is a function of how easily the use of all those methods, in tandem, would yield false beliefs about God. Arguably at least some such beliefs are safely formed or sustained, yielding knowledge.

2.2 Knowledge Defeat?

So far we have said nothing about what might *defeat* such knowledge, and contemporary epistemology often allows that knowledge can be lost, or prevented from being acquired, by the presence of defeaters. How shall we understand what such defeaters might involve, and how they operate?

A standard approach to defining defeat starts by appealing to intuitions about cases in which someone starts off with a rational or justified belief, but encounters new information which, if respected as relevant evidence, serves to reduce or defeat their justification. Thus, one who started off knowing could lose their justification and thereby their knowledge, even if they dismissed such new information and continued right on believing nevertheless. Beginning with this idea, some epistemologists countenance psychological or *mental state* defeaters, which do their defeating in virtue of being "held," mentally, by the subject. Some will regard having the relevant psychological state as defeating knowledge by defeating one's justification: If one gains information suggesting that one's evidence or reason E for believing that *p* is not as reliable or truthconducive as one had assumed, one often thereby loses the justification one had from E for believing that *p*. Similar views may invoke as a requirement of rationality that one not believe a proposition *p* when one also gains evidence for, or recognizes that one cannot rule out, the truth of another proposition which indicates that one's belief that *p* is false or unreliably formed (or sustained).[31]

In addition to mental state defeaters, some philosophers also admit that external facts can defeat even if the subject is unaware of them (Bergmann 2006, ch. 6; Lackey 2008, 44–45). Some think of these as *normative* defeaters, that is, a

---

[31] That the defeating proposition may indicate either falsity or unreliability means that it could be either a "rebutting" or an "undercutting" defeater, respectively. See Pollock (1986) for more.

doubt or belief which a subject *ought* to have (given the evidence or information available to that subject: Lackey 2008, 45 fn. 21), whereas others don't
require that one ought to believe them for them to defeat one's knowledge
(Klein 1971). While the above gloss permits these defeaters to be false propositions, since one's evidence might support a falsehood, such defeaters are more
often regarded as truths.[32] Thus, some endorse *factual* defeaters, namely, a true
proposition, which, if added to one's beliefs or one's evidence, would render
the belief in question unjustified. Though it is often left unsaid just what this
involves, it presumably involves the idea that adding a defeating true proposition D to one's evidence E for *p* significantly lowers, or would lower, the
probability of *p*, even if one does not yet believe D. At the very least, the conditional probability of *p* on E and D is less than its conditional probability on
E alone: $\Pr(p \mid E\&D) < \Pr(p \mid E)$.

A major problem, however, is that it is quite unclear how to model these
intuitive ideas, in terms of defeat of knowledge, in either an internalist and
externalist framework (Lasonen-Aarnio 2010; Baker-Hytch and Benton 2015).
If defeat is to be modeled probabilistically, and a defeater's contribution to a
belief's justification is understood in terms of how it affects one's evidence,
then much depends on what exactly counts as part of one's evidence, and how
propositions become part of one's evidence set. If knowing *p* makes *p* part
of one's evidence, then no proposition added to it will lower *p*'s probability, for the probability of *p* on a set that includes *p* is 1, whereas if knowing
p doesn't automatically make *p* part of one's evidence, we need a principled
way of explaining when and why one's knowledge does count as part of it.[33]
This feature of defeat also makes it hard to motivate the idea behind factual
or normative defeat, on which facts of which one isn't apprised, or which
one doesn't yet believe, could do any probability-lowering work (cf. Goldberg
2016 and Benton 2016). But the most promising accounts of the evidence-for

---

[32] Indeed, for any case in which one's evidence supports a falsehood which ought to be believed,
one might defer to the *fact that* one's evidence supports this as the relevant defeater: In this
way, false normative defeaters reduce to factual defeaters after all.

[33] The difficulty is captured especially well by those writing on E = K, though it does not depend
on that view: cf. Dietz and Hawthorne (2023, sect. 1.1): "Suppose we ask which hypothesis
about whodunnit is best supported by a particular detective's evidence at a particular time. If
they know the murder happened at noon and that Jones was asleep at noon, that is surely part of
their evidence – in this case exculpatory evidence regarding Jones. And if they don't know that
Jones was asleep when the murder happened, then that fact is surely not part of their evidence.
If we proceed as if, despite being known, the fact that Jones was asleep at noon was not part
of the detective's evidence, we would seem to be ignoring something that is fairly obvious,
namely that the detective's evidence is incompatible with the hypothesis that Jones committed
the murder at noon. And inclusion of such facts as evidence in the situation when they are
unknown would lead us to overestimate what the detective's evidence rules out."

relation are accounts of probability raising, particularly Bayesian frameworks for updating.

In particular, for externalists, it is quite unclear how, if one knows because one's belief is true and was initially formed by a reliable or safe method, that would change simply because one might encounter new information that putatively defeats it. Any information suggesting that one's belief that *p* was less than reliably formed, or is false, is misleading when one knows *p*, and being given misleading information does not in itself convert the (initially safe) process or method by which one formed the belief into an unsafe one. If I know by (reliable or safe) sensory perception that the items in front of me are red, being told that they are illuminated by red lights might (on the one hand) instill doubt in me because it suggests that my belief-forming process was unreliable. With such doubt, I should perhaps drop the belief that they're red, for it seems unreasonable to believe that my belief-forming faculty of vision is unreliable in this case while also nevertheless persisting in believing this on its basis. But (on the other hand) if receiving that testimony about red lighting did not induce such doubt, or if I dismissed such testimony as misleading or irrelevant, the process by which I formed and retain the belief presumably remains safe, at least under one important description: Safely formed beliefs do not become unsafe simply by dismissing false testimony as misleading.[34]

Other scenarios may seem more plausible to many: suppose I am at the pub enjoying a drink with my friend Blake. But while we are there, I receive a text from his wife indicating that Blake is elsewhere. In this case, even though that text might, given someone else's (weaker) evidence, undermine their justification for a belief about Blake's whereabouts, I can appropriately dismiss this as misleading evidence precisely because I know he is at the pub with me. Similarly, after buying a new home and moving in, you might receive postal mail at the address with someone else's name on it. This isn't, for you, evidence that someone else lives there, and it needn't defeat your knowledge that only you and your family live there. But of course, it might well be such evidence for someone else who doesn't know much about whose residence it is. So proponents of defeat owe us an account of why some sorts of new information count as important evidence and must defeat one's knowledge (whether or not one treats it as probative evidence), whereas other sorts of evidence do not. But

---

[34] An example from an externalist virtue epistemology (Sosa 2006, 2021, 18–20), on which knowledge is a belief which is accurate because adroit, and thus apt, on analogy with an archer whose shot hits the target because it was competently taken in the weather conditions they faced: Such a shot is not made less apt simply because someone told them that the weather conditions were different than they in fact were, or because someone (falsely) insinuated that their shot was less than competently taken.

it is proving extraordinarily hard to provide such an account. In the meantime, many philosophers have become pessimists about knowledge defeat.[35]

Even if an adequate account of knowledge defeat can be given, it need not doom the possibility of knowledge of theism or of some facts about God. Take the main routes into such knowledge adumbrated in Section 2.1, namely, by examining theistic arguments, or testimony, or religious experience. Most evaluators of theistic arguments also end up becoming aware of significant objections to such arguments, as well as counterarguments, such as from the problem of evil, or from divine hiddenness, or religious disagreement, arguments sometimes formulated in support of atheism, other times used to support the charge that theistic belief is (or can be) irrational even if true. But then most real-world cases of theism susceptible to defeat involve awareness of such putative defeaters from these arguments. In many such cases a theist will be able to discern what they take to be flaws in such arguments, particularly if their own beliefs are based on consideration of theistic arguments. Similarly, theists who initially believe by trusting someone's testimony usually also come to learn through that process that many others believe differently, or that relying solely on an individual's testimony might subject them to accidents of social location. But such theists can often remain rational by finding further sources of evidence which they find, on balance, nevertheless supportive of theism (though often they do not find such, and they might rationally drop their beliefs).

Diffusing such defeaters (sometimes called, inelegantly, having a "defeater defeater") presumably can restore one's overall belief-sustaining method as safe if it had become unsafe. What is more, many theists, however they initially formed their belief, will not accept a bare version of theism, but some more specific version which includes explanations of why there would be, say, suffering, or hiddenness, or religious disagreement. And given these more specific theistic commitments, such would-be defeating information is accommodated. That is, if their theism (T) also predicts the putatively defeating information (D), then D doesn't disconfirm or defeat T. Rather, D confirms it: For given D, the probability of T goes up rather than down when T is an expanded hypothesis that includes D. (Put differently, D confirms theistic hypotheses of the form T&D, which include D.)[36]

---

[35] Lasonen-Aarnio (2010, 2014), Greco (2010, Ch. 10), and Baker-Hytch and Benton (2015). Perhaps the most promising account of externalist defeat is Kelp (2023).

[36] "Even though evil is evidence against the existence of God, it does not follow that evil is evidence against Christianity. In fact, not only is evil not evidence against Christianity, evil is evidence *for* Christianity. Christianity entails the existence of evil, so the discovery of evil must confirm Christianity. It may seem strange that the horrors that disconfirm theism confirm Christianity, but it shouldn't. Consider the horror that an innocent man was unjustly crucified. Such a horror is bad news for theism, but good news for Christianity." Benton, Hawthorne,

Yet, because many judge that propositional knowledge about God's existence is not plausible (e.g., DeRose 2018), let's briefly sketch some ways to make good on, or otherwise explain, that judgment even within an externalist framework. First, the judgment of (mostly) nonknowledge is predictable, precisely because we cannot expect to have access to or understanding of the safe methods or reliable processes by which those who do know come to have that knowledge. Only those whose experience of God is so well established and reinforced will feel in a position to judge confidently that they know God exists, or even, to know that they know it. But this higher-order knowledge of whether (and how) one knows may not be very common; we will discuss this further in Sections 3 and 4. For all that though, it can be that one knows some *p*, such as that God exists, while not being very confident that one knows that one knows *p*. This is perhaps why some theistic traditions stress that knowledge by faith is contrasted with the phenomenal certainty of knowledge by sight, or that now we only see as in a (bad) mirror dimly, but after death we may see as "face to face."

Second, if we accept the possibility of knowledge defeat, we might propose that most will feel the pressure, in the face of so many potential defeaters, to say that religious belief is at best justified or rational, rather than knowledge, particularly because one suspects there are some defeaters about which one does not see what evidence or arguments might disarm them. Indeed, in some such cases, the defeaters may rob these individuals of justification or rationality for their beliefs altogether. (In the next section, I consider some such objections to theism from religious disagreement.)

Finally, beliefs about theism might often seem to share a feature of lottery beliefs. Many judge that one cannot know that a given lottery ticket in a large fair lottery is a losing ticket, even though one might believe, given the overwhelmingly high probability of that ticket losing, that it will lose (see Williamson 2000, 58–59, 246ff.; Hawthorne 2004, Chap. 1).[37] It might be that belief that God exists (or doesn't exist) can feel, from the inside, much like that case, where it can, for some, feel overwhelmingly likely given one's evidence or one's belief-forming (and sustaining) processes that the belief is true, yet one cannot shake the salient doubt that this belief might nevertheless be false. A major difference for lottery beliefs, of course, is that the salient possibility is imposed simply by the probabilistic structure of lotteries, where each

---

and Isaacs (2016, 8). As we acknowledge, there may remain problems owing to its low prior probability (see 2016, 8–9).

[37] Safety theorists have a nice explanation of why: Believing solely based on statistical probability in a fair lottery is a method for which one has a false belief in a similar case, namely, the nearby world in which that ticket happens to win.

ticket has the same chance of winning; whereas for theists, the salient doubt might be due to any number of factors, including just that the truth of theism isn't easily settled and there are plenty of naturalistic explanations of religiosity.

2.3 Disagreement and Defeatism

Some have urged that theistic beliefs are subject to serious objections owing to pervasive disagreement over religious worldviews, particularly *inter*religious disagreement between religious adherents, as well as *extra*religious disagreement between atheists, agnostics, and theists or religious adherents more broadly. The doubts generated by such disagreements, as well as from more typical counterarguments from suffering, are often thought to defeat any justification that the typical theist might have for her beliefs.[38] Given this situation, theists sometimes speak of their beliefs in terms of *faith*, often understood (in both philosophy as well as mainstream culture) as a weaker attitude of commitment which one may hold while lacking knowledge or even justified or rational theistic beliefs. (I postpone an account of faith until Section 5.)

Goldberg (2014 and 2021) argues at length that pervasive, systematic, and entrenched disagreements over religion generate defeaters for theists, robbing their beliefs of justification. Though I expressed some doubts about knowledge defeat Section 2.2, the remainder of this section takes up the matter from within a defeat framework.

Goldberg (2021, 66–68) argues that for the theist's positive beliefs about God (indeed, for religious beliefs in general), the pervasive and systematic disagreements we find over them are good reasons to accept the following claim:

> BAD PROSPECTS   The prospects that one oneself has reached the truth in matters of systematically contested religious belief are not good.

And if so, then it is easily argued:

> DEFEATING DOUBT   One has good grounds for doubting whether one has arrived at the truth in matters of systematically contested religious belief.

Importantly, Goldberg thinks that BAD PROSPECTS generates a problem for theists even if, as an externalist approach insists, their belief-forming methods are

---

[38] Though arguably a theist can know purely from testimony even despite such disagreements: see Baker-Hytch (2018).

reliable or safe, and so on. This is because he thinks that "one is never justified in believing anything through a process *one has adequate (undefeated) reasons to regard as not sufficiently likely to attain truth*" (2021, 69).[39]

Why is the existence of pervasive and systematic disagreement over theism a good reason to accept BAD PROSPECTS? Goldberg argues thus:

> it includes some *peer disagreement*; it has persisted despite the efforts of various groups at conversion (forced and otherwise), proselytization, conversation, and argumentation aimed at getting others around to one's own religious views, and despite the fact that so many people (many of whom are at least as well-off, epistemically, as one oneself on the matter at hand) are extremely motivated to get it right (given the rewards they anticipate if they do, or the punishments they anticipate if they don't); ... So on any given matter on which one's own belief is in the decided minority, where there are smart and otherwise knowledgeable people on the other side(s), where the disagreement has been persistent, and where one can't explain away all of the opposition, the chance that one is right are not particularly good. (Goldberg 2021, 71)

The force of the objection should be clear. If one accepts that those with whom one disagrees over theism have largely the same evidence, and have at least as good an ability to assess it, and are honestly motivated in their assessment, this perhaps should lead one to worry that one's own beliefs are untrue.

I do not have space to enter into these matters in the way they deserve,[40] so I shall have to register just a few objections. First, it is entirely unclear why we should suppose that disagreers over theism would tend to have largely the same evidence or be "at least as well-off, epistemically." Indeed, what counts as evidence is itself in dispute; but then one cannot easily appeal to this mess as if it supports only one side of the disagreement. Second, Goldberg argues that such disagreement supports BAD PROSPECTS, which generates defeaters for religious believers only, but not for, say, atheists (2021, 60, 86–88). Yet given this comparison, any appeal to the relevant sort of extrareligious disagreement (disagreement between the religious and "nones") will have to concede that, far from this being a matter on which religious belief "is in the decided minority," study after study show that those with religious beliefs, historically and today, constitute a strong global majority (many studies also show that the monotheistic traditions still make up a majority across the world). Looked at this way,

---

[39] Thus, Goldberg is assuming a hybrid account of justification, externalist about the belief-forming process but also requiring that the subject lack defeating higher-level doubts about one's belief-forming process that are not themselves defeated; cf. Bergmann (2006). For concerns about any such account, see Baker-Hytch and Benton (2015, 45–55).

[40] See Pittard (2020) for the most sustained discussion.

there is substantial extrareligious *agreement* in favor of some religious reality, and arguably broad agreement favoring monotheism.[41]

Third, while it might be that some facts about disagreement should give the complacent and uninformed religious believer some doubts, it seems likely that most arrive at and then sustain their beliefs while fully aware of such disagreements. And if one's religious views predict or explain why there would be systematic disagreements of the sort in question, and nevertheless can argue to their own satisfaction that their beliefs are correct,[42] then far from it constituting a defeater, such disagreements plausibly support their religious beliefs rather than count against them. For example, if a particular theistic tradition teaches that humanity is very likely to fall into such disputes and error, and that their theistic tradition won't be uniformly accepted, a theist of that tradition not only has a "defeater defeater"; these facts about entrenched disagreement *confirm* their brand of theism. (As mentioned earlier in Section 2.2, the probability of theism, $Pr(T)$, goes up rather than down because when T is an expanded hypothesis that includes D, $Pr(T|D) > Pr(T)$, because $Pr(T\&D|D) > Pr(T\&D)$.)

For these sorts of reasons then, I find such arguments from religious disagreements, made in objection to all theistic belief, to be too sweeping to be feasible. Compatible with this, however, is the possibility that many theists who have not carefully considered features of religious disagreement are overlooking defeaters or counterevidence, and more generally, considering such factors may appropriately lead such theists to reduce their confidence or hold their beliefs with more humility.

3 Epistemology Pluralized

The previous section examined propositional knowledge and how, on the assumption that God exists, one might acquire propositional knowledge about God on a broadly externalist conception. We noted that it might be difficult to gain (and sustain) such beliefs as knowledge, but that there is no principled reason to deny that it is possible or even quite common.

Yet knowing facts about God is not the only epistemic relation of interest, particularly to religious adherents of many theistic traditions. Theists often talk

---

[41] Put more formally, if $\neg p$ is evidence for a hypothesis H, then p is evidence for $\neg$H. So if broad (extra-)religious disagreement would be evidence against a religious hypothesis, then broad agreement on the matter is evidence for it. Note this is not to endorse a *consensus gentium* argument for theism; for discussion of that argument, see Kelly (2011) and Zagzebski (2012, 69–71 and 185ff).

[42] Perhaps, as MacIntyre (1988) suggests, an adherent of a tradition can handle systematic disagreements by citing considerations that would explain why a rival tradition fails to meet insurmountable difficulties.

of knowing God in some more relational sense, one which often coincides with trusting or putting faith in God. Many theists (and philosophical theologians) claim such ideas as important without clarifying how these relations are to be understood. Fortunately, recent epistemology has developed accounts of other sorts of knowledge which can be illuminating for religious epistemology.

3.1 Objectual and Practical Knowledge

Some philosophers argue that there are other sorts of knowledge that deserve to fall under epistemological theorizing but that are not reducible to propositional knowledge.[43] Though some philosophers argue that such putative knowledge is thus reducible, or that it should be explained away as not really a part of epistemology, I shall not adjudicate those debates here. For if such knowledge is somehow reducible to propositional knowledge, then the ideas adumbrated in the last previous section may be applied anew here; and insofar as our ordinary ascriptions of such knowledge reveal that we accept that we often stand in such cognitive relations, those applications are likely to be sufficiently nonskeptical. Our present interest is in identifying these other notions of knowledge, to examine how they may or may not apply to knowledge of God.

We sometimes claim that someone knows someone, or knows a city, or even knows a field of study. In English, these have a uniform grammatical construction, "S knows NP," where S stands for an individual subject, and NP stands for a noun-phrase such as a name, phrase, or definite description ("She knows Juan." "They know English literature." "He knows Boston." "She knows the Department Chair.") These knowledge ascriptions seem to invoke a relation which isn't simply a set of propositions known about the person, city, or domain of study, though having such knowledge typically involves a lot of propositional knowledge. The difference, it seems, is that such knowledge ascriptions require a certain amount of first-hand experiential contact, even an ongoing familiarity, with the "object," and thus sometimes this idea is called *objectual* knowledge or even *thing*-knowledge (e.g., Farkas 2019; Duncan 2020; Kukla 2023).[44]

Relatedly, philosophers have sometimes argued that sensory perception can provide one with *qualitative* or "what-it-is-like" knowledge, such as what one

---

[43] That is, they would be a knowledge-like (or broadly "epistemic") relation that cannot be analyzed or defined solely in terms of propositional knowledge.

[44] Such distinctions owe something to Bertrand Russell (1910/1998 [1912], Ch. 5), who importantly distinguished knowledge "by acquaintance" from knowledge "by description"; but his internalism assumes we are only (directly) acquainted with our own mental states, and thus his examples of someone who "knew" Bismarck ends up conflating what we are trying to distinguish, namely: (what came to be called) qualitative knowledge and knowing someone in the interpersonal sense (about which more below).

learns when one has experienced (and can remember) the color red, as might happen for someone who previously lacked color vision but suddenly has acquired it.[45] Such objectual or qualitative knowledge makes sense of the phenomena of suddenly recognizing more often tokens of the object type after one has attended to and remembered its distinctive qualities, where again this involves a sort of perceptual familiarity. The phenomenon is all too common: For example, it often happens when one has begun shopping for a new car, attending to a certain model and its many features and details, that one suddenly begins to notice that kind of car far more often than one used to do. A perhaps similar example is when one automatically recognizes a musical melody one has heard before, perhaps even being able to sing along to it, even if one cannot name it or place where one last heard it, without knowing how to represent the melody in musical notation, and so on.

Importantly then, objectual or qualitative knowledge requires special experiential conditions. One cannot count as knowing Boston, in the relevant sense, simply by having read a lot about it or studied maps of it; one must have experienced Boston by visiting it and exploring it, learning about it in that way.[46] This experience seems required to provide one the sort of understanding which gives one epistemic authority, even though for many of these places and objects one can, of course, know them more or less well. Significantly, characterizing such knowledge defies easy classification purely in terms of propositional knowledge; in particular, propositional knowledge can normally be transmitted from someone else via testimony, but objectual or qualitative knowledge do not seem like they could be acquired purely through testimony from those who have had the requisite experience.

In connection with these ideas, philosophers often draw a distinction between perceptually based *de re* knowledge – knowing, *about something*, that it is such-and-such – and *de dicto* knowledge, namely: propositional knowledge of

---

[45] See Nagel (1974), and Jackson (1986) for influential discussions; cf. Stump (2010, Ch. 4), who draws on Jackson to argue for her notion of "Franciscan" knowledge, discussed in what follows.

[46] Could one gain objectual knowledge of Boston (or practical, knowledge-how, discussed on the next page) through virtual simulations that imitate Boston (or allow one to practice the skill)? I think not; but this negative answer is compatible with two concessions. First, that such virtual experiences can help one gain some nearby knowledge or know-how: namely, an acquaintance or know-how with the (very phenomenally similar) "object," namely, the simulation of the real thing. And second, that someone learning such technologically mediated imitations typically knows them much *better* than someone who merely has gained much propositional knowledge about it by testimony (such as reading in books). One could thereby know it (say, Boston) better without having proper objectual knowledge of it, just like one could know many propositions about someone without having interpersonal knowledge as sketched in Section 3.2. (Thanks to a referee for raising this question.)

a fact, even a fact about that same something. Yet *de re* and *de dicto* knowledge, involving the same object, can come apart. A clear case is given by Wolterstorff:

> Suppose that one is in the city of Lansing and is reliably told that the city in which one finds oneself is the capital of the state of Michigan, but one doesn't know that the city is Lansing, nor does one know the name of the city that is the capital of Michigan. Then one knows, *about* the city in which one finds oneself, namely, Lansing, that it is the capital of the state of Michigan, but one doesn't know *that* Lansing is the capital of the state of Michigan (2021, 215–216).

Thus, one can know, *of* the city one is in (*de re*), that it is the capital, without knowing (*de dicto*) that *Lansing is the capital of Michigan*. Likewise, one might learn (*de dicto*) that *Lansing is the capital of Michigan* without knowing *de re*, of the city one is in (because one happens to be driving through it and one missed seeing the sign), that it is Lansing. Similarly, one might have *de re* qualitative knowledge of Lansing (e.g., what it is like to navigate its streets or experience its architecture, say) without *de dicto* knowledge of propositions related to such qualitative features; or again, one might have such *de dicto* knowledge about Lansing without having any *de re* qualitative knowledge about it.[47]

Another kind of knowledge is *practical* knowledge or *knowledge-how*, a kind of skill at doing something.[48] Knowing how to ride a bike, or throw a football, or to type on a keyboard, all seem to be skills that involve a sort of cognition. But crucially, they also require a set of experiences built up through practice, and so similarly, they cannot be learned at second hand by believing another's testimony. Some views of objectual knowledge appeal to practical knowledge to make sense of it: they might require repeated interactions which earn one a firsthand familiarity with the object, which facilitates practical knowledge of how to interact with it.

Recently, some philosophers have also inquired into what it is to know someone (Stump 2010, ch. 3; Talbert 2015; Benton 2017), sometimes drawing on the already mentioned notions of objectual knowledge and practical knowledge. In particular, we might ask what is the relation expressed when we talk of knowing someone "personally"?[49] Stump (2010) argues for a closely related idea, contrasting the propositional knowledge recently emphasized by analytic

---

[47] Burge (1977) argues that *de re* belief is more fundamental than *de dicto* belief; cf. Moss (forthcoming), arguing that all knowledge-that is knowledge-of.

[48] See Ryle (1949); Stanley and Williamson (2001); Stanley (2011); and Farkas (2016).

[49] As said in English. Many other languages have a dedicated lexical item for interpersonal knowledge: *saber* in Spanish, *kennen* in German, *makir* in modern Hebrew, *rènshi* in Chinese, and so on.

philosophers (what she calls "Dominican" knowledge) with what she calls "Franciscan" knowledge, including "Franciscan knowledge of persons."

Stump initially characterizes Franciscan knowledge negatively, simply in terms of "irreducibility to knowledge *that*," acknowledging that she cannot give a set of necessary and sufficient conditions (2010, 47–48, 51). Stump suggests that we can grasp what Franciscan knowledge is by drawing on Jackson's (1982, 1986) cases of Mary, wherein Mary's new experience gains her a qualitative, what-it-is-like knowledge of the color red (Stump 2010, 52). Taking the original Mary case as inspiration, Stump invites us to consider a different Mary, imprisoned her whole life in a room wherein she learns all manner of facts about the world and others only through third-personal factual accounts, but without "any personal interactions of an unmediated and direct sort with another person," the kind "in which one can say 'you' to another person." Mary would, upon emerging from this room to meet her loving mother for the first time, begin to gain much qualitative, what-it-is-like knowledge of being touched and loved by another person, but also a kind of personal, Franciscan knowledge: She would begin to know her mother (2010, 52). This Franciscan knowledge of persons then is distinguished from other kinds of knowledge about persons, including propositional ("Dominican") knowledge (2010, 47–51).

Stump sometimes claims that "the direct and immediate encounter with another human," in "face-to-face … interpersonal interactions" is crucial for gaining Franciscan knowledge of someone (2010, 52–53); but she also claims, immediately thereafter, that "any direct causal contact between the knower and the person known" is "not necessary" to gain it (2010, 53). This is because Stump thinks that Franciscan knowledge of persons can be acquired primarily by way of narratives, the hearing of which constitutes a kind of second-personal engagement with the person(s) of the narrative. However, because of these emphases, Stump seems to be committed to the idea that one can "know" (personally, in her Franciscan sense) people who no longer exist such as dead people, as well as fictional characters who are not even people (and who, if they "exist," are abstract objects, not persons: see 2010, 53, 78–79). Thus, Stump must deny the highly intuitive idea that knowing someone requires that they at least be both a person, and also (presently) exist.[50] For how could one (even

---

[50] One might build upon a Single-Premise Closure principle (Hawthorne 2004, 34), where "knows$_i$" labels the interpersonal knowledge I shall articulate later in this section:

> EXISTS: Necessarily, if S knows that S knows$_i$ R, competently deduces that R exists, and thereby comes to believe that R exists, while retaining knowledge that S knows$_i$ R throughout, then S knows that R exists.

Franciscanly) know someone who is neither a person nor an existing thing? Furthermore, comparing a case of S knowing personally someone who exists, with that of S knowing (in Stump's Franciscan sense) a fictional character, reveals that the former relation is both more natural and a relation of genuine epistemic interest: Knowing an existing person brings a kind of cognitive connection with the social world of actual persons.[51] So while Stump offers us a route in, I think we can articulate a much more satisfying interpersonal epistemology.

3.2 Interpersonal Knowledge

We shall inquire then into what it is to know someone, a matter of philosophical as well as of public social interest.[52] Importantly, it can be easy to conflate knowledge *about* someone, with knowing someone personally (which I will call *interpersonal* knowledge). Knowledge about someone could be propositional (of facts about them), or it could be objectual or qualitative, having observed "what-they-are-like." Thus, we should be alert to the possibility that such interpersonal knowledge might often involve these, while also not being reducible to them.

Let's start with some commonsense judgments about knowledge and human persons, which situate the issues and allow for important distinctions. First, we can acquire propositional knowledge about other persons, where such facts might be learned in the typical ways in which we learn facts about the empirical or impersonal world: for example, by sense perception, by testimony, or by some combination of these, including memory and reasoning. Second, a great many of those facts that we learn about people whom we've never met nor laid eyes on is learned through testimonial channels alone, including those mediated by technology. Third, we can know a lot about people we never meet or get to know personally. Fourth, we can also know others personally without knowing very many facts about them (and even while believing a great many falsehoods about them). And fifth, knowing someone personally is not transmissible by testimony in the way that propositional knowledge about someone is: One cannot come to know someone personally simply by learning a lot about them from those who do know them personally.

But such propositional knowledge that one knows, may sometimes be hard to come by, depending on the subject in question and one's context of knowing. Indeed, I give counterexamples to it later in Section 3.3. See Benton (2018a, 425–426) for more.

[51] Recently, Stump acknowledged that there might be a problem here, at least with entirely fictional characters (2017, 187 nn. 23, 24; cf. 2010, 521 n. 98); but she does not consider it further.

[52] For recent popular books, see, e.g., Gladwell (2019) and especially Brooks (2023).

Crucial distinctions are needed even at this early juncture. For we often are willing to claim a special sort of knowledge about someone based entirely on perceptual observation of them, of the sort which their own acquaintances and friends might be typically thought to have. Thus, I can learn what you look like, your mood patterns and mannerisms, your habits and preferences, all by sense perception. Such qualitative knowledge is knowledge *about* you, so in that sense, it involves experiencing you. Observing and remembering such qualitative features of you will often be an ideal way to learn many more facts about you, and thus perception can issue in propositional knowledge as well.

Yet someone could acquire a great deal of such personal qualitative (and propositional) knowledge about you without ever interacting with you. Such knowledge can be had by perceiving you undetected, as a spy or private investigator might do. We are sometimes inclined to call such qualities a kind of "personal" knowledge of you, particularly if they are largely private or intimate details about you. While we might deem either intimate facts or other qualitative features of you "personal" knowledge, they do not suffice for knowing someone in the personal or relational sense.[53] This is illustrated by the following case: Juan and Julia work at the same company, and have gone to the same large committee meetings, over many years. They know each other's names and institutional roles, and know many other facts about each other; but they know all this from other sources, or by overhearing conversations each is having with other people. They hear each other offer suggestions in meetings, but they've never addressed each other individually in conversation or other messages. They know much about each other, but intuitively, Julia and Juan do not know each other in our interpersonal sense.

Central to the difference between interpersonal knowledge, and other sorts of knowledge about someone, is a sort of reciprocal, second-personal treatment, in which each person treats the other person as a subject rather than an impersonal object: as an "I" to a particular "you." To get what this would amount to, we may distinguish three grades of personal involvement, the first two of which demarcate ways that, on the one hand, we can acquire propositional knowledge about someone, but, on the other hand, are insufficient for interpersonal knowledge:

---

[53] A somewhat similar view thinks of second-personal/acquaintance knowledge as a kind of success in seeing someone as a person, particularly through a kind of pattern perception (Green 2012, 2015). This sort of qualitative knowledge is not reducible to propositions known about the person, and can facilitate joint attention when interacting, and so on. These are ways of knowing someone in quite intimate and personal ways; but they do not suffice for knowing someone interpersonally, as defined here. My view is closer to Talbert's (2015).

First grade (*de dicto*): propositional knowledge of one gained without perceptual experience of them (especially, for example, through testimony).

Second grade (*de percipio*): propositional or qualitative knowledge about someone gained by perceptual access to them (even if mediated by technology).[54] (Benton 2017, §2)

Through the testimonial means delineated by the first grade, we are capable of learning a great many facts about someone. And through the perceptual means of the second grade, we can learn facts as well as gain familiarity with qualitative features of an individual, such as their mannerisms, mood patterns, or what they look like, qualities which plausibly do not reduce to facts about which one might gain propositional knowledge. These two grades offer one knowledge-*wh*, by which one might be able to answer a *wh*-question, such as *Where is Emily?* or *Who is Keyser Söze?*[55] Thus, the more you know about someone, the better positioned you are to answer a range of such *wh*-questions. We tend to associate rising through these grades with learning more about someone: Learning facts and qualitative features of someone through perceptual access to them typically makes one more epistemically authoritative about them than if one merely had a lot of propositional knowledge about them learned from testimony.

Through the first two grades we can learn much about someone without at all interacting with them; and thus they appear to be insufficient for coming to know someone personally. Moreover, knowing someone personally is not transmissible by testimony in the way that propositional knowledge about someone is. Thus, there is a *third* grade of personal involvement which includes how one treats the other person, namely: as a subject rather than a mere object (Talbert 2015, 194–197; Benton 2017, 820–821). Each of the first two grades needn't involve treating the one about whom one is learning in any way at all, whereas this grade requires that one treat the person in a "you"-like manner. Because it is second-personal in its mode of interacting, we might call this the *de te* or *interpersonal* grade of involvement:

---

[54] Is such *de percipio* knowledge about someone equivalent to *de re* knowledge (cf. Section 3.1) about them? Although *de re* knowledge is typically grounded by sensory perception, they aren't equivalent, because one could have *de re* knowledge without having such perceptual access. I can know of the world's tallest man (whoever he is) that he's over seven feet tall, even if I've never had perceptual access to him. I can have such *de re* knowledge about him (as well as *de dicto* knowledge of that fact) even if I don't know (*de dicto*) who he is.

[55] Cf. Stanley (2011, 36–37); Benton (2017, 818–819).

> *Interpersonal* grade (*de te*): A treatment by a subject *S* toward its recipient
> *R* is *second-personal* in virtue of *S* treating *R* as a subject (an individ-
> ual "you"), where *S* offers some of *S*'s own thoughts, words, attitudes,
> or emotions to *R*, and *S* is, or largely intends to be, attentive to *R*'s
> thoughts, words, attitudes, or emotions.

This interpersonal grade is best understood in terms of engaging with another
person in the cognitive modality of "I–you," such that one presents one's
thoughts, words, attitudes, or emotions, for example in conversation or facial
gestures or even eye contact, relating to them typically in reciprocal fashion.[56]
Note that learning how to engage in such treatment will itself be a kind of
practical knowledge, particularly where such practical knowledge-how will
become sensitive to features of their personality, needs, the context of interactions, and more. Thus, interpersonal knowledge plausibly depends on a finely
developed (interpersonal) practical knowledge.[57]

One might suspect that we can know someone in a personal way, even if not
quite in the intended interpersonal sense, without *reciprocal* second-personal
treatment. For example, suppose that two school children, Ada and Liam, are
sitting in their classroom with their classmates on the first day of a new school
year, waiting to meet their new teacher, Ms. Chandra. She walks into the room
and addresses the class as a whole, giving them an inspiring talk about their
year ahead. Unfortunately, Liam was hidden out of Ms. Chandra's sight by a
large pillar in the classroom, though she could see Ada and most of the other
students. At this point, before there are any introductions of students to the
teacher, what shall we say about who here "knows" the teacher, including what
sort of knowledge they might have? Clearly, most students can identify Ms.
Chandra as their teacher, having gained qualitative knowledge of her face, her
voice, her demeanor, and so on. They may have acquired much propositional
knowledge about her intentions, her hopes for their year, her wardrobe, and so
on. To the extent that Ms. Chandra has seen and is now able to recognize many
of her students' faces and thus identify them as her students, she may also have
gained some qualitative knowledge of them, although she does not have such

---

[56] For cognitively developed individuals, this blending of the *de se* and *de te* normally involves
deploying conceptual and linguistic resources involving the (grammatical) first- and second-
person. But it might be possible even for infants to engage in comparable abilities, particularly
in the early stages of attachment through face-to-face interactions, including coy and clowning
playful behavior (see Reddy 2008). Indeed, much work in interpersonal neurobiology suggests
that proper cognitive development depends on such interactions (e.g., Siegel 2020). Cf. also
Green (2012).

[57] At least in cognitively developed individuals. It may be that proto versions of it are available
for infants, or dogs, and so on.

qualitative knowledge of Liam yet. Ms. Chandra's speech to her students has, of course, treated them each as a "you," yet it was given to them collectively, in the plural: for "you all, my students". Should we say that these are enough to enable them to count as knowing her "personally"?

I think not, which is why the "I–you" interactions must be with a particular individual as the "you," and that they be reciprocated. Until Ms. Chandra has interacted with an individual student where they've introduced themselves and they've spoken *to* each other in response to one another, it feels wrong to claim that they have interpersonal knowledge.[58] So arguably then, to know someone in this interpersonal sense (abbreviated "$know_i$"), one must experience, and engage in, interpersonal encounters with the following necessary conditions:

ENCOUNTER: S knows$_i$ R only if (i) S has had reciprocal causal contact with R, in which (ii) S treats R second-personally, and (iii) R treats S second-personally.[59]

Clauses (ii) and (iii) require each person to treat the other second-personally, and (i) requires the contact between two individuals to be *reciprocal*, which it will be insofar as each shares with the other some of their own thoughts, words, attitudes, or emotions in response to the other. Thus, to facilitate the acquisition of interpersonal knowledge, these encounters must be intentionally two-way. For one would not come to know$_i$ someone by treating them as a "you" in a variety of ways specified by the interpersonal grade, but where they fail to notice, receive, and respond in kind to one's interpersonal efforts.[60] Interacting with one another as "I" to a singular "you" is needed to gain knowledge$_i$ through mutually relating to one another.[61]

---

[58] A test: Would the police seeking to question someone who knows a particular person S, or a lawyer seeking a character witness or someone to vouch for S, be satisfied with the sort of exposure or learning given by the Ms. Chandra episode?

[59] Cf. Benton (2017, 822ff). I eschew sufficient conditions for knowledge$_i$, partly because I think it unclear when and how knowledge$_i$ might be lost. I also suspect there may be no sufficient conditions for knowledge$_i$ (for related parallel concerns with respect to propositional knowledge, see Williamson (2000, especially Ch. 2)).

[60] Our focus is two-way personal relationships. But many relationships are shaped and even constituted in an asymmetrical way, particularly in caregiving, or in child-rearing relationships (cf. Lindemann 2014 on "holding," and Dalmiya 2016 on care ethics); *mutatis* for cruel or abusive relationships. I want to insist that one can know others "personally" in many such scenarios, in both directions; but the availability of empathy or memory, and so on will change the way such relationships, and even the identities of the individuals, develop. For theorists who want to build respect or empathy into the required second-personal treatment, there will be many cases of one-sided knowing$_i$.

[61] Cf. Gómez (1996, 2005, 2022, *a.o.*), who argues for *second person intentional relations*: "First person relations involve computations of the type 'I → X,' where 'I' stands for some (primitive, nonreflective) representation of the perceiver, '→' stands for a directed activity, and 'X' stands

Note that Encounter's clause (i) is not redundant given (ii) and (iii), because the latter conditions can be met without fulfilling the former. Suppose that Maud writes a letter to someone, Jim, whom she has never met or interacted with. Coincidentally, Jim also writes a letter to Maud. But neither letter is received by the other (perhaps this is repeated, with letters never being received). Arguably clauses (ii) and (iii) are fulfilled, but not (i); and intuitively, they do not yet know each other personally. This judgment remains intuitive when we add to the case that each letter is received and read, but neither Jim nor Maud respond to the other's letter.[62] Relatedly, for the case of an intercepted letter: If Peter receives Maud's letter addressed to and intended for Jim, he does not thereby come to know Maud personally, nor does Maud come to know Peter personally (*mutatis mutandis* for, say, a conversational eavesdropper). In this case, none of clauses (i)–(iii) are fulfilled.[63] In short, fulfilling

---

for an object. Third person relations must in turn involve computations of the kind 'O →
X,' where 'O' is an organism different from the perceiver and X the object of its activity.
Accordingly, a second person relation would be as follows: 'O → I.' That is, second person
relations involve a combination of the distinctive elements of first and third person relations.
Furthermore, in the case of relations like seeing or attending, a second person relation involves
a *bidirectionality* not present in either first or third person ones: Given 'I look at Y' and 'Y looks
at I,' something like 'I ⟷ Y' follows, where a new, bidirectional kind of intentional relation
is introduced. . . . Thus, second person intentional relations, as I have defined them, represent
an integration of first and third person intentional relations that gives rise to a new kind of
bidirectional intentionality" (Gómez 1996, 130). Cf. also his "Attention contact" component
of joint attention, in Gómez (2005, especially 66).

[62] Notice that becoming acquainted with a fictional character by reading a novel involves a kind
of contact with both the "mind" of the character, and the mind of the author; but there is no
reciprocation, nor (I take it) does the reader treat the character or author second-personally, and
thus Encounter is failed. Contrast Stump's (2010, Chs. 3–4) account, which allows one to
know ("Franciscanly") a fictional character.

[63] What about a speaker/lecturer presenting to a large group? The speaker takes a broader second-
person (plural) perspective toward other persons, but the attentiveness and reciprocation from
the audience (even if there is Q&A) is minimal and when present, it is very one-sided; and so
arguably, in some cases, either clause (i) or (iii) (or both) are not fulfilled.
     Could people come to know$_i$ each other through entirely second-person plural interactions?
Imagine a group of six people who meet and get to know each other by standing in a circle,
facing each other; each speaks directly to all of the others in the group, each revealing much
about themselves and responding to the others, in an *I*–(plural)*you* back-and-forth conversation. But no person is ever singled out in an *I*–(singular)*you* interchange. Does this fail to count
as interpersonal given that it doesn't involved one-on-one interactions? Given the definitions
given earlier, it seems like it should not count as interpersonal in my sense; yet it still seems
like people could come to know each other ("personally") in this way. Perhaps the case is
underdescribed, however. For even if no speaker ever explicitly refers to or uses a singular-
you, whenever one of the six in the conversation responds to or picks up on something said
by an earlier speaker, they are, in some minimal way, acknowledging and treating them as an
individual, such that their thoughts and attitudes (etc.) are offered *to*, and in recognition *of*, that
person, as well as being offered to the other four members; if so, a given act might contain
overlapping singular and plural second-personal treatments. Perhaps then such a case of plural interactions inevitably smuggles in some individualized treatment (even if never explicitly
addressed to them as a *you*). (Thanks to a referee for raising this question.)

ENCOUNTER ensures that the causal contact is reciprocal and taken up under second-personal terms.

If further motivation is needed for the significant role of both directions of such second-personal treatment, imagine a world where all its persons (minds) are capable of thinking first-personal "I" thoughts, and third-personal "he/she/they/it" thoughts, but lack the ability (and language) for "you" thoughts: In such a world, even though they might perceptually recognize others and learn facts about each other, it seems plausible that no one would count as knowing$_i$ anyone else, in no small part because they cannot relate to each other in a second-personal manner. Similarly, and secondly, we might imagine a different world where just *one* person has the needed second-personal ability but no one else does; plausibly that individual also fails to know others personally, because they lack the two-way reciprocal personal encounters needed to gain interpersonal knowledge. Finally, we might imagine a third world, in which there are *two* individuals with the needed second-personal ability, while all the remaining persons lack this ability (these latter having only first-personal and third-personal cognitive resources). But our two subjects are on different sides of the planet, and without any technological means to communicate (e.g., through writing) with the other, even if they know about the existence of the other person. It seems that even if our two subjects could recruit the help of those who cannot think or relate to others second-personally, they would be unable to mediate any second-personal attempts at communication, and thus it would not be possible for our two subjects, under these constrained conditions, to come to know$_i$ each other.

These features of ENCOUNTER, according to which the sorts of interactions needed are such that both parties have engaged in them, show important ways in which interpersonal knowledge is distinctive: Knowledge$_i$ is mind-dependent insofar as its object is itself another mind, and its reciprocal treatments make a difference to what is known, each of which are departures from standard ways of theorizing in propositional epistemology.[64] Such features might also suggest that knowledge$_i$ is symmetrical in structure:

SYMMETRY: *S* knows$_i$ *R* only if *R* knows$_i$ *S*.

SYMMETRY could be true even if it is common for people to know each other at different levels of intimacy; what it rules it out is the possibility that someone

---

[64] Hallmarks of mind-independence, and not altering or modifying the thing known, were stressed by the Oxford Realists against the idealists: see Cook Wilson (1926b, especially Part I, Ch. IV), Prichard (1909), and Marion (2000, especially 307–308).

could know$_i$ someone without them being known$_i$ by them, even minimally as an acquaintance, in return.[65] Yet, for most of what follows very little turns on accepting SYMMETRY, and it is enough to note that paradigm cases of knowledge$_i$ are symmetrical.

Having thus differentiated how we gain propositional and qualitative knowledge about someone and how we can come to know$_i$, one can nevertheless feel there is a strong connection between such knowledges, and perhaps something even incoherent about the idea that one could have knowledge$_i$ without some particular propositional or qualitative knowledge about someone. The next section considers the plausibility of some transparency principles relating knowledge$_i$ to propositional knowledge about them.

3.3 Interpersonal Knowledge and Its Limits

What is the relationship between propositional knowledge about a person and knowing$_i$ them, or even merely treating them second-personally? We might naturally suppose that knowing$_i$ someone involves knowing a privileged set of facts or qualitative attributes that are essential to knowing them, or at least essential to knowing them *well*. Our most common way of learning particular facts about someone else is by interacting with them, thereby facilitating our knowing$_i$ each other. And we also tend to assume that knowing$_i$ someone ought to automatically issue in propositional knowledge that they are known$_i$. Considering such cases can lead one to suppose that a strong transparency principle such as one of common knowledge, or a KK-style principle of knowing that one knows$_i$ another, is true:

COMMON K   If S knows$_i$ someone R, then S and R both know that they know$_i$ each other, and know that they know that they know$_i$ each other, and so on.[66]

KK$_i$ If S knows$_i$ someone R, then S knows that they know$_i$ R.

Or if not KK$_i$, it is natural to suppose that some weaker principle such as one of the following must hold:

LUMINOSITY K$_i$ If S knows$_i$ someone R, then S is in a position to know that they know$_i$ R.[67]

---

[65] See Benton (2017, 826–827) for further reasons in support of SYMMETRY. Cf. Wolterstorff (2021, 224–226), on behalf of one-way knowing.
[66] Lederman (2017) casts doubt on common knowledge; see Immerman (2022) for a rejoinder.
[67] On Williamson's terminology (2000, Ch. 4), a condition C is *luminous* just in case whenever one is in C, one is in a position to know one is in C, whereas C is *absence-luminous*

BK$_i$ If S knows$_i$ someone R, then S believes that they know$_i$ R.

WEAK LUMINOSITY   If S knows$_i$ someone R, then S is in a position to believe (rationally) that they know$_i$ R.

Are any such principles correct? If not, how exactly does knowledge$_i$ relate to propositional knowledge?

Though most of our relationships, even among mere acquaintances, satisfy principles like these, the following counterexample suggests that even WEAK LUMINOSITY is false. Mary Jane knows$_i$ Peter Parker. And let us suppose, as might be so in an early stage of the story, that Mary Jane strongly doubts the existence of this high-flying superhero, Spiderman. Nevertheless, by knowing$_i$ Peter, Mary Jane thereby also knows$_i$ Spiderman. And this is so despite the fact that she might fail to believe that, and may even disbelieve that, Spiderman exists.[68] This case of Mary Jane thus falsifies WEAK LUMINOSITY, as well as each of its stronger counterparts, because Mary Jane knows$_i$ Spiderman but is not in a position to believe[69] (rationally) that she knows$_i$ Spiderman. (Those more classically inclined might instead adapt the case of Orlando and Rosalind/Ganymede from Shakespeare's *As You Like It*.)

Or at least, she is not in a position to believe this *under the guise* of him as Spiderman. So perhaps we should understand these principles as implicitly restricting the belief or knowledge under a relevant guise, along the lines of, for example:

WEAK LUMINOSITY*   If S knows$_i$ someone R (under the guise of S's beliefs about R), then S is in a position to believe (rationally, under that guise) that they know$_i$ R.

For Mary Jane surely still knows$_i$ Spiderman under the guise of Peter Parker. Yet even with such implicit restrictions to such principles, they seem false.

---

just in case whenever one is not in C, one is in a position to know that one is not in C; and he calls a condition *transparent* just in case it is both luminous and absence-luminous. Williamson argues against the luminosity of propositional knowledge, and of mental states more generally. Cf. also Sosa (2009, 2011, 2015, Chs. 3–4) on distinguishing object-level knowledge (what he calls "animal" knowledge) from higher-order, "reflective" knowledge (when one knows that one knows some proposition). Sosa's virtue epistemology is different from Williamson's knowledge-first approach, but they largely agree on the level distinctions and the nonluminosity of propositional knowledge.

[68] We get the same results with definite descriptions as opposed to names. Suppose Jan knows$_i$ her neighbor Eric. Eric is the author of the book *1984*. Jan doesn't believe Eric is an author, and even believes that *1984* has no single author (for some reason believing it to be group-authored). Nevertheless, Jan knows$_i$ the author of 1984.

[69] At least not without further evidence, plus some sort of Gestalt shift in how she has understood the evidence she already possesses.

Take a case where S, the would-be knower$_i$ of R, has suspended judgment about whether R still exists, as in the case of a lost loved one who (as it happens) is stranded on an island, never to be found. In such a case S will not be in a position to believe (rationally, under their guise or mode of presentation for R) that S (still) knows$_i$ R: Since one's judgment that one knows$_i$ another shifts to demurral upon learning of their death, it likewise calls for doubt when one does not know whether they live.[70] Or suppose that you've interacted in a second-personal manner, over many weeks, with someone online who, you realize, might instead be just an AI bot – where such a bot, let's suppose, doesn't count as a person. You could nevertheless, upon finally meeting in-person this online acquaintance for the first time, rightly judge that you've known$_i$ each other for some of the earlier period during which you had suspended judgment about whether you know$_i$ them. Thus, we find counterexamples even to WEAK LUMINOSITY*.[71]

So when S knows$_i$ R, this fact is not guaranteed to be known, believed, or even available to be rationally believed by S. Thus far our discussion substantiates the ideas of AUTONOMY and OPACITY:

AUTONOMY   One can know all manner of propositions about *R* without yet knowing$_i$ *R*; and one can know$_i$ *R* without knowing any particular set of truths about them (and without any specific qualitative knowledge of them).

OPACITY   One can know$_i$ someone *R* while failing to believe that one knows$_i$ *R* (under the relevant guise), and even while falsely believing (under a certain guise), that they do not exist.

In this way we find a significant parallel between propositional knowledge and interpersonal knowledge: Opacity for interpersonal knowledge is the analogue of nonluminosity for propositional knowledge (Williamson (2000, Ch. 4).[72]

This permits an error theory akin to a pragmatic (as opposed to semantic) explanation of our knowledge$_i$ ascribing behavior, including our natural inclination to think that knowledge$_i$ must be connected to some particular propositional or qualitative knowledge about someone. For while it is highly typical for us to acquire propositional or qualitative knowledge about someone gained by interacting with and getting to know them personally, and while we associate this knowledge with our relationship with them, particularly when asked to

---

[70] Cf. Craig (1991, 147); Benton (2017, 826).

[71] See Cullison (2010, 221) for a case of a lost loved one, as well as cases of relationships in his Turing Chat Room and Hallucination scenarios.

[72] Strictly, OPACITY is the analogue of non-WEAK LUMINOSITY for propositional knowledge.

substantiate how *well* we know someone, no particular propositional or qualitative knowledge about someone is essential for knowing$_i$ them. Moreover, the various sorts of knowledge we might have of someone can be *fragmented*,[73] such that one can have some propositional knowledge or qualitative knowledge about someone without knowing (under a particular guise) that one has it. Or, one can have such knowledge without it aligning in typical ways with the guises under which one knows$_i$ them. No such combination of knowledges, or how they are connected in one's "mental map" of someone, is essential to knowing$_i$ them. What is essential is reciprocal second-personal treatment, and the "shared worlds" this creates (Talbert 2015, 198ff.).

An interpersonal epistemology as sketched above illuminates a number of philosophical areas. Knowing$_i$ others, and the second-personal treatment it requires, informs work in moral psychology, empathy, and the interpersonal attitudes operative within valuable relationships such as friendships. These relationships typically involve cultivating dispositions to share one's own experiences, and listen to another's experiences, both of which can be important factors in diagnosing and addressing epistemic injustice (cf. Fricker 2007; Medina 2013). The richness of communicative content conveyed through narrating one's own experience likewise may contribute to an important but often overlooked role for an epistemology of narrative testimony (Fraser 2021). And such relationships typically include important roles for trust, loyalty, promising, or placing hope in another (cf. Martin 2019 on interpersonal hope, or Simpson 2023 on trust). While good friendships typically involve some form of benevolence or love, a further issue concerns the extent to which objectual knowledge, or the second-personal treatment which enables knowledge$_i$, makes possible certain forms of love.[74] In addition, in human affairs knowledge$_i$ seems to be presupposed by, and can also contribute to, our best accounts of forgiveness. Forgiveness is arguably normatively significant insofar as it alters the operative norms bearing on the interaction between the wronged and the wrongdoer (Warmke 2016; Green 2021). And forgiveness seems to be necessary for growth in healthy human relationships, since the paradigm cases of it involve a special form of second-personal treatment.[75] Though we cannot explore all these topics here, it seems clear that an epistemology of

---

[73] See Greco (2015a) for related discussion.

[74] Augustine argues that we cannot love individuals whom we do not know (*De Trinitate*, X.1–3; 1991, 286–298). Similarly, Scotus argues that singular cognition of someone is needed to love them (*De anima* q. 22, nn. 20–25; cf. *Questions on the Metaphysics of Aristotle*, VII, q. 15; Etzkorn and Wolter 1997, 254–265). Cf. Murdoch (2014 [1970], 27–29), and Mason (2020) for discussion; and also Kolodny (2003) and Setiya (2023).

[75] Pettigrove (2012) begins by focusing on the function of saying "I forgive you" to another.

interpersonal knowledge touches upon a broad spectrum of issues in moral psychology, social cognition, and human flourishing.

4 Knowledge(s) of God

The foregoing enables a straightforward application to how humans might acquire interpersonal knowledge (knowledge$_i$) of God. Put succinctly, those who treat God second-personally, as a *you* or *thou*, perhaps in prayer or worship or listening for the divine voice, plausibly facilitate divine reciprocation of such treatment, and if those conditions hold, such an individual will be on their way to acquiring knowledge$_i$ of God. A human's experience of this would be, of course, a distinctive sort of religious experience, not merely one of being (quasi-perceptually) appeared-to so as to rationalize the belief that God exists or that God loves them. Such interactions enable humans to gain a better grasp of what God is like, even if what is learned defies linguistic expression (see Keller 2018). And many religious people take themselves to have had such interpersonal interactions as part of their experiences of God (see Luhrmann (2012 and 2020) for two major anthropological studies).[76]

Some details are worth briefly exploring. Given that ENCOUNTER, discussed in Section 3.2, only gives necessary conditions for knowledge$_i$, it is unclear how many such interactions involving second-personal treatment suffice for knowing$_i$ God. At a minimum, if it only need involve one such reciprocation between a human and God, much turns on who first entered the interpersonal grade by treating the other second-personally. If God's self-revelation consists in communicating second-personally to an individual human, or even to all of humanity through nature or through sacred texts, then that human's response treating God as *you* or *thou* plausibly counts as a reciprocation, thereby meeting the necessary conditions of ENCOUNTER, even if God never responds in kind. However, if the human's second-personal treatment of God counts as the first relational overture, then God's reciprocation of it in second-personal terms would be needed to fulfill ENCOUNTER. (Some theists may want to insist on there being one-way knowing, by which God knows each of us even if we never respond, of a sort which is like knowledge$_i$ and not mere objectual or propositional omniscience. One such account would deny that there is any divine analogue of SYMMETRY from Section 3.2 even if it holds for human knowledge$_i$. Even if this view ends up being well-motivated, we should acknowledge that God nevertheless would lack knowledge$_i$ of many people,

[76] See also Baker and Zimmerman (2019), and Goldman (2019), on perceptual experience of God in the context of issues in cognitive science.

at least as knowledge$_i$ has been articulated here. See Benton (2018a, §4) for more.)

The present account of interpersonal knowledge also complicates the many epistemic relations one might bear toward God, for as I've suggested, even in human affairs such knowledges do not always march in lockstep together. First, as argued in Section 2, one might acquire propositional knowledge about God, such as about God's existence or attributes. But one could have such knowledge about divine facts without having objectual or qualitative knowledge of God, or practical knowledge of how to engage with God, or without yet knowing$_i$ God. For one might acquire it by purely intellectual means such as by accepting sound arguments, or by believing the testimony of someone else who knows it. Since propositional, objectual, and practical knowledge are distinct epistemic relations, one might also lack typical beliefs or propositional knowledge about God and nevertheless have a kind of objectual or qualitative knowledge of God. The next two sections consider detailed examples of this possibility.

4.1 Fragmentation for Nontheists

If God shows up to one in experience, one might thereby learn something experientially about what God is like. Importantly, however, it seems possible for one to acquire such qualitative knowledge without even believing under the guise or mode of presentation that it is *God* that one has experienced. Plantinga puts a similar point thus:

> It is even possible to believe [*de re*] of God that he exists and be an atheist: [e.g.] I encounter God in experience, believe of the thing that I encounter that it exists, but fail to believe that this thing I encounter is all-powerful or all-knowing or wholly good, or has created the world; and I also believe that there is nothing that has those properties. (Plantinga 2000, 294)

Perhaps in most cases of God providing a religious experience, it will be unmistakable that it is God. But I think we should not assume that the scenario sketched by Plantinga does not occur. Drawing on the resources of the previous section, we can articulate how someone might cognize or even treat God in particular ways without believing, under some guises, that God exists; and one might do so even while believing, under some guises, that there is no God.

Can one know$_i$, or at least relate to God second-personally, without even believing that God exists? J. L. Schellenberg (1993, 2015a, 2015b) argues for a negative answer to a nearby question, and uses this denial as support for a premise in a hiddenness argument for skepticism about traditional theism.

In its most succinct form, Schellenberg's argument runs:

(1) If a loving God exists, then there are no nonculpable nonbelievers.
(2) There are nonculpable nonbelievers.
So, (3) No loving God exists.

When spelled out more fully, his support for premise (1) concerns a defense of sub-premises, typically along the lines of one of the following:

> (4) If there is a perfectly loving God, all creatures capable of explicit and positively meaningful relationship with God who have not freely shut themselves off from God believe that God exists. (Schellenberg 2008, §2)
>
> (5) If for any capable finite person S and time t, God is open to being in a personal relationship with S at t, then for any capable finite person S and time t, it is not the case that S is at t nonresistantly in a state of nonbelief in relation to the proposition that God exists. (Schellenberg 2015a, 25)

Schellenberg's recent defense of such premises appeals to the following *general* principle about persons, their beliefs, and being open to relationship:

> *Not Open*   Necessarily, if a person A, without having brought about this condition through resistance of personal relationship with a person B, is at some time in a state of nonbelief in relation to the proposition that B exists, *where B at that time knows this and could ensure that A's nonbelief is at that time changed to belief*, then it is not the case that B is open at the time in question to having a personal relationship with A then. (Schellenberg 2015a, 23; cf. 2015b, 57)

Let us suppose, as seems highly plausible, that knowing$_i$ another, along the lines of interpersonal knowledge discussed in Section 3.2, counts as a personal relationship of the kind Schellenberg has in mind in *Not Open*.[77]

Recall, however, from our discussion in Section 3 that humans can know others personally while disbelieving, under a certain guise, that they exist. Recall the case of Mary Jane, who can believe that Spiderman does not exist even though she knows$_i$ Peter Parker (and believes that *Parker* exists).[78] Given this much, it should be clear that *Not Open*, which is supposed to be a fully general principle applying to all persons and what it is for them to be open to

---

[77]   Indeed, it is perhaps even a stronger relation than what Schellenberg needs; but if so, the point made next will show that his principle does not hold even when assuming this stronger relation.

[78]   Cullison (2010) offers counterexamples where a person A can continue in meaningful relationship with someone B, where A formerly believed B exists, but A now suspends judgment concerning B's existence (because A is not confident that B is still alive); cf. also points by J. Greco (2015b); Cuneo (2016, 57); and Stump (2017, 182). The present example, however, is different because Mary Jane does not even start off believing, under the right guise, that Spiderman exists.

personal relationship, is false. And since Schellenberg relies on *Not Open* to derive premises like (5), his hiddenness argument clearly fails.

This counterexample likewise calls into question passages where Schellenberg assumes that it is "impossible" to "do or experience any of the" myriad things "involved in a conscious, reciprocal relationship [with God] *if she does not believe that God exists*" (Schellenberg 2015a, 25). To repair his argument, Schellenberg would need to supplement it in order for his principle *Not Open* to be plausible: He would need to offer a guise theory which spells out under what guise or description one must believe that the person with whom one is in relationship exists. Yet this kind of repair seems out of reach, given that in Section 3 we found that interpersonal knowing is autonomous relative to any particular propositions known (or even believed) about the person, and that it can be opaque to us what knowledge we may have of someone. Such fragmentation of our knowledge is possible because the descriptions or guises under which we believe things about others, even about whether they exist, can be inaccurate even while we nevertheless do know, them.

4.2 God, the Good, and Guises

Yet how could someone experience or relate to God without the relevant beliefs? Plantinga's quote from the beginning of Section 4.1 gives a brief example, but what follows presents a more positive account.

On a common conception of God, God just is *the Good*, that is, God is the source and exemplar of all moral and aesthetic goodness, in the sense of "excellence." Anything which is excellent, such that it is worthy of our love and admiration, participates in and resembles the Good. As Robert M. Adams (1999, Ch. 1) articulates it: "If God is the Good itself, then the Good is not an abstract object but a concrete (though not a physical) individual. Indeed, it is a *person*, or importantly like a person" (1999, 14). Moreover, God is a being who is a lover, who desires our excellence and our participation in a loving relationship with God:

> [M]ost of the excellences that are most important to us, and of whose value we are most confident, are excellences of persons or of qualities or actions or works or lives or stories of persons. So if excellence consists in resembling or imaging a being that is the Good itself, nothing is more important to the role of the Good itself than that persons and their properties should be able to resemble or image it. That is obviously likelier to be possible if the Good itself is a person or importantly like a person. (Adams 1999, 42)[79]

---

[79] "A similar but doubtless shakier line of argument might be used to support the conclusion that the Good itself is also importantly like a *society* of persons, as claimed by the Christian doctrine

On this view, God is the Good and all beauty and goodness thereby emanate from and resemble God; and we should perhaps add to this picture that God draws us, much like a magnet, towards God's self. As John Hare puts it, "God is the ultimate good that is drawing us toward itself. . . the good is what draws us and deserves to draw us, other things being equal" (Hare 2007, 252–253).[80]

Relatedly, Aquinas held that everyone has a general but confused knowledge of God, for they know what goodness is, and yet for Aquinas, goodness (as well as perfect happiness) is really just the same thing as God. Thus Aquinas argues that

> To know that God exists in a common and confused way is sown in us by nature, inasmuch as God is man's beatitude. For man naturally desires happiness, and what is naturally desired by man must be naturally known to him. This, however, is not simply to know that God exists; just as to know that someone is approaching is not the same as to know that Peter is approaching, even though it is Peter who is approaching (*Summa Theologiae* I, q. 2, a. 1, ad 1; cited in Brent 2017)

And again:

> Goodness is found above all with God, for goodness follows upon desirability. Now, all beings desire their perfection. . . In desiring its own perfection everything desires God himself, since, as we noted, the perfections of all things somehow image the divine existence. And thus among beings desirous of God, some know him in himself. . . others know his goodness as participated somewhere or other, and this is open even to sense-knowledge; while other beings, without any knowledge, desire by nature, guided to their goal by some higher being with knowledge (*Summa Theologiae* I, q. 6, a. 1, c)

On this God-as-the-Good[81] view, God can be conceived either as a person or importantly like a person (perhaps a "personal non-person"; for more, see Page 2019).

---

of the Trinity. For we confidently ascribe excellences to social systems and to interpersonal relationships, and we value those excellences highly. So if we think excellence consists in resembling or imaging the Good itself, we seem to be committed to the belief that societies and social relationships can resemble or image the Good itself. And that is likelier to be possible if the Good itself is importantly like a society" (Adams 1999, 42 fn. 40).

[80] For the idea of God as magnet (particularly in Aristotle), see Hare (2007, Ch. 1, especially 15–16, 60–65 and 251ff). Cf. Murdoch on the Good as magnet: "Good is indefinable . . . because of the infinite difficulty of the task of apprehending a magnetic but inexhaustible reality" (Murdoch 2014 [1970], 41); "The image of the Good as a transcendent magnetic centre seems to me the least corruptible and most realistic picture for us to use in our reflections on the moral life" (p. 73; though Murdoch disavows it as divine). Relatedly, for reference magnetism (metaphysical and linguistic) about moral rightness for moral realists, see Dunaway (2020).

[81] Cf. also the Cambridge Platonist, Ralph Cudworth (discussed by Taliaferro 2017, 210–212); Wainwright (2002, 113–114, 118 and fn. 27); Stump (2017, 183).

If God is the Good in the sense sketched, perhaps a theist can insist that the agnostic or avowed atheist who feeds the hungry, cares for the poor and the sick, welcomes the stranger, visits the imprisoned, and so on might well, by such actions, acquire at least an objectual knowledge of God; for they are pursuing the moral good in loving their neighbor. They might even be relating in crucial ways to God while nevertheless they believe that they do not believe, or that they disbelieve, there is a God.[82] Yet avowals of nonbelief or disbelief aside, their actions and emotions, insofar as they are pursuing the Good, might reveal something like a suppressed belief in or awareness of divine reality: Since propositional knowledge is nonluminous, we can sometimes know that *p* while not being positioned to know that we know it, and even while it being highly improbable on one's evidence that one knows it (Williamson 2014).

Even further, it is plausible that sometimes we know that *p* while being wrong about whether we believe *p*, that is, one's explicit beliefs (what one is willing to affirm as true) might differ from one's implicit beliefs (cf. D. Greco 2015a). Everyday examples make this plausible: Someone might be an avowed anti-sexist or anti-racist, but their residual tacit beliefs in fact remain sexist or racist. Their affective reactions and behaviors are the main evidence of their implicit or tacit beliefs. (This distinction is used more broadly in epistemology, for example, as an important part of Moore's defense of common sense against idealists and others, namely: observe their behavior.[83]) So we sometimes might be wrong about what we say we believe.

This might be plausible for those who deny that God exists under the guise of their theistic conception, while nevertheless accepting that something or someone is worthy of one's awe and gratitude, is behind morality and justice, and so on.[84] For others who do not make such denials, it may be that they can do God's will or relate to God as the Good by acting in certain ways, particularly if their actions aim to serve or promote the Good, while accepting (or merely being open to the possibility) that God is real. Such individuals could at least have objectual knowledge of God, and even begin the process

---

[82] Christian theists might appeal here to Matt. 25:31–46: "Truly I tell you, just as you did it to the least of these, you did it to me"; cf. Matt. 7:21–23; and 1 John 4:7–8: "love is from God; everyone who loves is born of God and knows God. Whoever does not love does not know God, for God is love."

[83] Moore (1959, 41); Lazerowitz (1942) called this inconsistency between what some philosophers claim to believe, and what their actions reveal about what they know, "Moore's paradox," though that label later came to mean more narrowly that assertions of the form "*p* and I don't believe/know that *p*" are bizarre even though their conjuncts could be true.

[84] Cf. Baillie (1939, Ch. 2), arguing that some atheists "deny God at the top of their minds, but believe in the bottom of their hearts."

of coming to know$_i$ God without yet knowing that God exists.[85] Even if that may seem implausible, at the very least we should allow that such actions can be ways of relating to the Good, namely God, which somehow can enable (perhaps at a later time, and under an accurate guise) treating God second-personally, and eventually knowing$_i$ God. Perhaps the most apt model of this is an infant who, through its ongoing interactions, acquires qualitative and inter-personal familiarity with its mother, and thus *knows* her. But it knows her well in these ways long before being able to describe or conceptualize her as a *you*; only much later does the child gain accurate beliefs and language for express-ing the (descriptive) guises under which they can think about, refer to, and communicate about their mother. In this sense, interpersonal treatment and the sort of interactive knowledge(s) it enables can precede knowing$_i$ someone in the mature ways characteristic of most of our relationships. Yet, for all that, one correctly judges retrospectively that the infant was coming to know its mother; perhaps something comparable can occur for many people with respect to God.

4.3 Fragmentation for Theists

Take now the case of the avowed theist who has had such experiences and rightly believes that they are experiences of God; and so they believe and per-haps even know that God exists. Nevertheless, they might not yet have (or even approach) knowledge$_i$ of God, insofar as they might fail to engage God second-personally, as divine *you* or *thou*; and thus such knowledge$_i$ is discrete from the other epistemic relations. Of course, many such theists will have under-taken treating God as such, for example through prayer or worship, and if so, they have begun their side of the reciprocal second-personal treatment. God's responding in kind would, if Encounter is correct, seem to be needed for one to acquire knowledge$_i$.

Indeed, since it seems possible to be relating in second-personal terms toward God without realizing that one is doing so, many theists may wonder about the status of their epistemic relation to God, and desire a second-order knowledge or certainty concerning it. This anxious theist will resonate with John Wesley's desire, written in his journal before his conversion experience:

---

[85] Compare Aquinas on concurrence, *Summa Theologiae* II.II q. 2 a. 5–7; and Stump (2010, 163–64, 2011) for discussion of divine presence. The present project perhaps is prefigured in Aquinas's notions of connatural knowledge and divine concurrence; but I shall let Aquinas experts sort out how well his views coincide with any that I've argued for here.

I want that faith which none can have without knowing that he hath it (though many *imagine* they have it, who have it not).[86]

Wesley here invokes, on the one hand, the desire for some sort of assurance of one's epistemic (and redeemed) relation to God,[87] while, on the other hand, allowing that one could be mistaken about being in that relation.

Now we have not yet given a proper gloss on what *faith* might be, and we shall postpone that until the next section. But suppose for now we interpret Wesley's notion of faith in terms of knowledge$_i$, or at least in terms of one's efforts at second-personal treatment toward God. On that construal, Wesley wants not just to know$_i$ (or be on his way to knowing$_i$) God, but also to know that he knows$_i$ God. Yet recall that OPACITY – not always knowing or even believing that one knows$_i$ – is a structural feature common to other mental states, insofar as propositional knowledge is nonluminous. Recognizing and embracing that we don't always know when we know some facts, or don't always know that we know$_i$ someone, can at least temper the expectation that religious conviction must always involve a feeling of "firm and certain knowledge." [88]

This framework offers an interesting upshot for epistemic issues related to religious disagreements. For someone could relate to God second-personally and even know$_i$ God while believing a number of false claims about God. This has ramifications for epistemological issues involving interreligious disagreements between say Jews, Christians, and Muslims. Those in the broadly monotheistic religions can, in principle, bear structurally similar epistemic relations to God despite their disagreements over significant core theological (or moral) commitments. Thus, many Christians and Muslims and Jews might refer to, know (qualitative or propositional) about, and know$_i$ the same God, though of course their reasons for such commitments will draw on, and be

---

[86] Wesley continues that "whosoever hath it" is "freed from sin . . . freed from fear . . . [and] freed from doubt" (Wesley's Journal, January 31, 1738: 1988, 216). I do not think this passage suggests that Wesley must think there is a distinct kind of faith, enjoying these features; rather, he means to be highlighting that he craves a certain experiential and epistemic validation of the faith he already has.

[87] Compare Cook Wilson (1926a, 853): "But in some subjects we have an impulse, which cannot be stilled, for what is called direct knowledge. If we think of the existence of our friends; it is the 'direct knowledge' we want: merely inferential knowledge seems a poor affair. . . . We don't want merely inferred friends. Could we possibly be satisfied with an inferred God?" Cook Wilson goes on to argue (anticipating similar anti-luminosity ideas to those developed by Williamson a century later) against the idea that we will always be aware of what is in our consciousness and acting on it (citing our often implicit knowledge of valid inference, of causation, and of our own self); he also argues that certain emotions such as gratitude, awe, and reverence might be unconsciously directed at God (1926a, 854–865).

[88] As Calvin repeatedly claims in *Institutes* III.ii.7, and III.ii.17.

motivated in part by, different claims (and where such claims are false, of course, they thereby lack propositional knowledge).[89] That is, interreligious disagreement over the nature and attributes of God, or of God's actions in historical events, or of who count as God's speakers or prophets, and so on, need not affect the possibility of some of them acquiring and maintaining propositional or qualitative knowledge about God. Moreover, such disagreements need not affect the possibility of knowledge$_i$ of God, for these religious adherents, for such knowledge$_i$, can withstand much falsity in one's beliefs.[90] Thus, their interreligious disagreements, which are often substantial and the source of much discord, are nevertheless subsidiary to the several shared epistemic and interpersonal relations which they might corporately share toward God.

To sum up how far we've come: In Section 3, I argued that one might well have not just propositional knowledge about someone, but a sort of objectual knowledge, practical knowledge, and even interpersonal knowledge of them. Although the best cases of knowing others typically bring with them all of such knowledges at once (including, usually, knowledge that they exist), these are discrete relations and so they can be fragmented. That such fragmentation is possible becomes clear once we realize that knowledge of others is often had under guises or beliefs which do not track all the connections between who they are and how we regard whom it is we know. Then, in this section, I've argued that if there is a God, similar epistemic relations might be had when the other is God, particularly on the conception of God as the Good, to which most of us bear some epistemic relations insofar as our moral or aesthetic sensibilities tend (even imperfectly) to track goodness. Thus, even here objectual knowledge of goodness can come apart from one's beliefs or knowledge about its object (God). This yields interesting and perhaps surprising results about one's explicit judgments that one has (or lacks) any such knowledge of God, and for how to conceive of various monotheistic believers' epistemic relations to God.

5 Interpersonal Faith

What are the connections between the foregoing ideas concerning knowledge about someone, interpersonally knowing someone, and what it is to have faith

---

[89] Sameness of linguistic reference is perhaps easier to secure than the further idea that they all *worship* the same God. For linguistic matters of reference and meaning, see Sullivan (2012, 2015), and especially Keller (2018); for arguments about worship, see Bogardus and Urban (2017).

[90] Just as *intra*religious disagreement between Christians, or between Muslims, need not rob one of knowledge, or on the occasions where it does so, it need not block one's second-personal efforts toward God, nor God's responsiveness. See Benton (2021, especially sect. 2.4). Cf. also Dormandy (2021) for arguments that engaging across such disagreements can be epistemically fruitful.

in someone? And how might we then conceptualize what faith in someone like God involves?

In Section 3, I argued that knowing a lot (propositionally or qualitatively) *about* someone is neither necessary nor sufficient for knowing$_i$ of the sort that figures in interpersonal relationships. It's just that the typical, paradigm cases of knowing$_i$ someone bring with it a decent amount of such propositional knowledge about them, and repeated interactions tend to increase such knowledge, giving each knower a kind of "mental map" of the person they are getting to know$_i$. Here I shall explore how the interpersonal epistemology developed earlier provides a useful point of departure for talking about faith in another person.[91]

5.1 Faith in Another as a Virtue

Having faith in another typically involves a way of being on good terms with them. One can, of course, know$_i$ someone without being on good terms with them, and without having or putting faith in them. One can also know$_i$ someone while being on good enough terms with them, but where one's relationship is superficial and one might only put faith in them with respect to certain domains. (One might put faith in one's postal carrier to deliver the mail, but to do little else.) Yet, insofar as benevolent regard of the sort needed to love another is part of being on minimally good terms with someone, and insofar as trusting them on a certain range of matters is also a way of being on good terms with them, love for and trust in others are important for the ethical ways in which we treat others.[92] Such love and trust are also prescribed in many theistic traditions as how one ought to orient oneself to God; in addition, and significantly, in many traditions faith in God is regarded as a virtue.

Here I shall seek to develop the notion of we may call *interpersonal faith in God*,[93] giving an account of such faith as a virtue. Such an account may be understood in terms of three desiderata. First, such an account should make

---

[91] I shall not try to enter the growing debate over the exact nature of faith, or its many manifestations. For helpful discussion, see Buchak (2012, 2014), Howard-Snyder (2013), Kvanvig (2018, chs. 2–3), Swinburne (2005), or Jackson (2023).

[92] Note that Aristotle's remarks on friendship come close to the reciprocal structure of ENCOUNTER from Section 3.2, adding in the mutual recognition of bearing good will: *Nicomachean Ethics* Bk. 8.2, especially 1156a1–5, and Bk. 9.5, especially 1166b30–35. Thus, the elements in play here are related to what makes for friendship (indeed, this makes sense of why we often find it easiest to put faith in our friends). Though I shall not discuss the notion of friendship with God, such a relation would have to be asymmetrical in crucial ways. On valuable asymmetrical friendships, see Mooney and Williams (2017).

[93] Cf. the account of *relational faith* in McKaughan (2017); Howard-Snyder and McKaughan (2022); cf. also Morgan (2022, especially 22–26). For more see Section 5.2.

good on the idea that faith involves a way of relating to God as a person, or at least in a personal way (as discussed in Section 4). Second, such an account should show how, as a virtue, faith in God exhibits some structural similarity to other virtues. And third, such an account should illustrate how, when a virtuous faith is mature, it explains what it is to trust God in terms of how we relate to God as a person, and how such relating to God goes beyond merely putting optimal confidence in particular outcomes for which one trusts God. (Developing this third desideratum will be a chief aim of Section 5.2.)

If faith is rightly called a virtue, then it would be unsurprising if faith exhibited a comparable structure to other virtues, particularly the moral virtues. Following a tradition broadly espoused by both Aristotle and Kant, one can be deemed to act virtuously only when one acts for the right sort of reason. Similarly then, interpersonal faith is a virtue only when it is directed toward, and responsive to, the right sort of object: namely, a person. In the case of theistic faith, the right sort of object is the Divine person (or the Divine personal being, if God is a nonperson).

Such a schematic structure can be given more precision. Following Christine Swanton (2003), we might define virtue as "a good quality of character, more specifically a disposition to respond to, or acknowledge, items within its field or fields in an excellent or good enough way," where a virtue's *field* "consists of those items which are the sphere(s) of concern of the virtue, and to which the agent should respond in line with the virtue's demands" (2003, 19–20). On this approach to understanding virtue, courage, for example, has as its field (at least) a fear of harm, as well as goods only gained through risk. But the courageous person is disposed, in an environment or context demanding action in the face of that fear, so to act, where the intentional object of one's courageous action would be securing the good recognized to be worthy of acting for despite one's fear. Similarly, honesty might have as its field the good of truthtelling, and a particular interlocutor's need to hear the truth, where those goods are aimed at by the person who speaks honestly. On this approach to virtue, we can delineate certain *relational virtues*, such as filial piety, or the virtue of friendship, where such a virtue has as its sphere one's relationship with one's parent or one's friend. As Sungwoo Um (2021) argues, these relational virtues are "required for an individual as an excellent participant of the given type of intimate relationship," relationships which of course seem to presuppose knowing₁ one another (personally). "Intimate relationships generate normative demands, responsibilities, or expectations on their participants since intimates have a great influence on each other's flourishing in a special way"; and thus a person who has such a relational virtue will exhibit a "proper sensitivity to those normative demands and appropriate modes of responsiveness to them" (Um 2021, 96).

Arguably, possession of virtues will structure what reasons one has to act (Saunders 2021). The virtue or character trait of generosity, for example, explains what reasons a generous person has for acting in certain scenarios, whereas the ungenerous person would fail to have those reasons in such scenarios. And this seems all the more plausible when it comes to relational virtues. If interpersonal faith is to be a relational virtue in this sense, then it likewise will structure the moral psychology of the faithful person, by providing them with reasons which make rational and motivate certain actions, particularly actions which affect one's relationship with the other. Faith in someone with whom one has a flourishing relationship will presumably dispose one to treat them in terms of relational excellence, exhibiting pleasantness, friendliness, generosity, good temper, modesty, and so on.[94] Exhibiting many of these relational virtues involves caring for and even loving the other person.

For the person with faith in God, this will involve acquiring particular (and ongoing) reasons to engage in acts of faith, for example through devotional activities of prayer to and worship of God, and acts of serving and caring for others out of love for God. Their faith in God thus issues in a wide range of these actions which, over time, develop into a kind of practical knowledge, namely: a knowledge-how to express their faith in God, where engaging in such know-how will not only be ways of interacting with and on behalf of other persons, but also will be ways of relating to God.[95] And these deployments of such knowledge-how in action in turn make possible further reasons for perhaps new actions. Some such reasons might even be given, received, and perhaps only comprehended under the second-personal guise of relating to God: perceptual capacities to hear God's voice may be engaged and conceptualized in the second-person, such as when one comes to feel God's directing one, as a "you," to undertake a specific action.[96] Or similarly, when one might feel God's loving response in terms of God speaking or conveying that "I forgive you." Thus, these modes of relating plausibly facilitate the reception and function of forgiveness, which, at least for Christians, is central to God's love.

---

[94] As in Aristotle's virtues as a mean, *Nicomachean Ethics*, Bk. II. Perhaps one could even make room for our notion of interpersonal faith in this framework, as a mean between the vices of naivete and cynicism. (Thanks to Daniel Rubio for this suggestion.)

[95] See Sliwa (2018). See also Rea (2018, 133ff.) on acquiring the kind of skill involved with experiencing the presence of God.

[96] See Simpson (2023, Ch. 4) on whether trust should be construed as making available second-personal reasons (to trust their testimony, for example). Cf. Anscombe's notion of faith in a person, and of believing a person (their say-so), in Anscombe (2008, Chs. 1–2).

Since forgiveness is normatively significant in that it alters the operative norms bearing on the interaction between the wronged and the wrongdoer,[97] the relational interactions constitutive of interpersonal faith in God play a fundamental role.

5.2 State of Love and Trust

For all that has been said thus far, one might be disposed to relate second-personally to God, take part in actions through and for the sake of loving God, and develop one's cognitive resources to recognize and respond to reasons given by thus relating to God. But one might do all this while nevertheless falling short of *trusting* God as a person of faith ought to do. This is important insofar as faith even in other humans seems to require at least a kind of minimal trust in them on some matter (even if highly restricted, as noted by the postal carrier example from the previous section). Such trust is conceptualized as expressing more than mere reliance on another, for it involves a way of relating to them. Since faith in someone involves a kind of concern for the person and a sort of trust in them, we might think of interpersonal faith as a dispositional state of love and trust.

Interpersonal faith in God will at least involve the three-place relation of someone placing trust in God on some particular matter (*S* trusts God with respect to *p*). Such faith in God, then, is a disposition which includes or gives rise to an attitude toward God, which involves trust in God with respect to some domain(s); and this enables an account of how such faith can be less or more virtuous. Someone with less than mature faith in God might trust God on some matters, but only in a few areas of their lives: Their immaturity of faith would be due, at least in part, to being unable to trust God when it comes to key cherished domains. As such faith grows and matures, such trust will not manifest itself in terms of an attitude only toward particular propositions or outcomes for which one trusts God. When most mature, faith in God would be more thoroughgoing than this, insofar as the one trusted is (typically) assumed to be more capable and reliable than any other agent, who oversees all events and eventualities, and who has our long-term best interests in mind. In these typical cases, mature faith is a bit like what Howard-Snyder (2017, 56) calls *relational* faith: a disposition to have such a trusting attitude toward a person, *as an X*, where "X" predicates an attribute of the person in virtue of which they are trustworthy. Given the present approach to interpersonal faith in God, this would be a disposition to trust God, construed as the Divine *thou* or *you*, where

---

[97] See especially Warmke (2016, 2017), and Strabbing (2017).

X involves perhaps some of the assumed attributes of God: as *more capable and reliable than any other agent*, as *one who has our long-term best interests in mind*, or even (in an Anselmian philosophical key) as *one who is most worthy of worship*.

However, the core notion of interpersonal faith need not involve such attribute predication. For one might trust God with respect to whatever comes one's way, or with how things occur elsewhere in the world, without predicating any relevant theological attributes of God which might make such trust fitting or rational,[98] in the same way that a small child might be disposed to trust a parent or other adult (especially one that they know$_i$) without having in mind an attribute of theirs which rationalizes such trust. Thus I suggest that a person has such fully mature faith in God, then, when they are able and disposed to say (or pray) to God something like: "whatever happens, I trust *you*." Thus, the field of trust for interpersonal faith in God will be very wide, far wider than simply trusting God for specific possibilities or outcomes desired. It is perhaps not quite as wide as the "whatever" quantifier just used; for the field of propositions or outcomes about which one trusts God does not float free from the sorts of outcomes which one can rationally expect or hope from God. The field of trust is thus restricted somewhat by one's theology. Nevertheless, the hallmark of maturing in one's faith is the movement from trust as merely a three-place relation (between a person and God with respect to specific possibilities) to a two-place relation (between a person and God, and open-ended with respect to all manner of domains).[99]

The second-personal structure of such matured faith, once expressible in terms of the two-place relation "I trust you," is constituted in part by second-personal trust. In typical mature cases, this is made psychologically possible owing to a recognition of God's love for one, and such trust is given (even imperfectly) as part of one's love for God. Developing and sustaining such mature faith depends on cultivating the practices and actions which enable both relational knowledge-how and a deepening reliance on God.[100] Indeed, such trust should be strengthened in accordance with how well, or deeply, one comes to interact with and know$_i$ God.[101]

---

[98] My approach is descriptive rather than normative here: I am not aiming to give an account of interpersonal faith in terms of what mental states or evidence might make it most rational or fitting.

[99] See Simpson (2023, 10–11) for trust as fundamentally a two-place relation, and 156ff. on such trust in God; cf. also Morgan (2022, 10–12, 93–95).

[100] Such practices and habits, of course, are embodied, and also enable one to cultivate theistic belief itself. See Ritchie (2021) for more.

[101] Cf. Green (2015) for an attachment-theoretic account of how some people may be hindered in such relational development, affecting even the possibility of their believing theism.

On this gloss we thus can distinguish merely *having* faith from being faith*ful*. Given this approach to what fully mature faith involves, it is easy to see how (what we often call) a *lack* of faith can just be a weak or immature faith, one which is related to fear and trust in the following way. Following Adams (1984), we can say that trusting another person, particularly when that person is God, should be understood in part "as a sort of freedom from fear. It is a conceptual truth that if I fear that God will let me down, I do not entirely trust Him. Conversely, perfect trust in God would free us from that fear, and from many others" (1984, 10). To qualify this, we should perhaps insist that the freedom in question isn't from the feeling of fear, as much as a freedom from *allowing* such fear to dominate one's emotional mindset or control one's decisions. For a person trying to lead a life of faith, Adams thinks this fear exhibiting a lack of trust can manifest itself in an inability to relinquish a kind of "lust for *control* of" one's "own life and its circumstances" (Adams 1984, 11). And what makes faith in God such a weighty commitment is that

> [t]he supreme threat to our control, however, is God Himself. In Christian faith we are invited to trust a person so much greater than ourselves that we cannot understand Him very fully. We have to trust His power and goodness in general, without having a blueprint of what He is going to do in detail. This is very disturbing because it entails a loss of our control of our own lives. (Adams 1984, 12)

Not only that, "God demands of us the greatest trust, the acceptance of the most complete dependence. In death He confronts each of us with a total loss of control over our own destiny" (Adams 1984, 14).

Insofar as we must depend on others in personal relationships, not only to get some of what we want (which would, were it the only aim, be purely manipulative) but also to attain relational goals involving their cooperation, our uncertainty about exactly how other people will act makes it possible, Adams thinks, "to *depend* on another person in a way that is much more personal. It enables the other person to be more truly other" (Adams 1984, 13). In this way, the most mature faith in God will be faith in the Divine personal being, to whom one is related in love and trusting dependence, as well as in adoration and worship. Maturing in such theistic faith will involve widening the domain of events over which one trusts God, along with adjusting one's desires when the outcomes one asks for do not obtain. The acknowledged dependence on God, which the faithful stance requires, is one which allows that God is someone with whom the faithful person must cooperate in order to understand and reach their shared relational goals. Yet such faith also would involve a dependence on God, to whom one presumably must surrender control in order to be guided by

God. For God would be one whom the faithful person strives to love, and who, they plausibly must believe, loves us far more than we could fully understand.

As articulated here, interpersonal faith is importantly connected to love for and trust in God, and such trust is construed as second-personal in structure. Significantly, engaging in or developing such faith does not much depend on having any of the knowledges (propositional, objectual, practical, or interpersonal) discussed in earlier sections. Thus, we find yet again the possibility that the epistemic or fideistic relations an individual might stand in toward God may be fragmented from one another. The various distinctions drawn by our interpersonal epistemology and this relational notion of faith thus open up a variety of ways that God may seem *hidden* from us. The sort of certainty or epistemically optimal confidence often desired by believers is an idea which tends to collapse these distinctions, flattening them in such a way that knowledge and certainty concerning God's existence and love for us is the main cognitive expectation for persons of faith. Often, these are conjoined with related implicit ideas about religious experience according to which one will always know when God is present or speaking to one. But the considerations explored here should give us pause about these all too common notions of religious epistemology. One might be well-related to God in faith, or through knowledge (or knowledge$_i$), while struggling with doubt about whether one is so related, or whether one knows various claims about God, or about whether one knows$_i$ God. One might know a lot of truths about God while not yet knowing$_i$, or having much faith in, God. Or one might put faith in God without knowing$_i$, or feeling like one knows$_i$, God. One might even have (at least an immature) faith in God without having much practical knowledge of how to interact with or recognize God. Insofar as our cognitive and relational capacities are ones we do not always have excellent grasp of, we should expect God to feel hidden.[102] Yet even if so, the sorts of second-personal treatment and skill required to have and grow in faith in God can still be engaged. And, for most faithful individuals we may plausibly assume that they likewise will have acquired some such knowledge, and typically, that those who have developed a mature faith in God also know$_i$, and rightly judge that they know$_i$, God.

5.3 Conclusion

Mainstream epistemology in recent decades broadened its interests from focusing on analyzing propositional knowledge and the structure of epistemic

---

[102] Similar issues apply even to human interactions, depending on how we construe the epistemic relations of joint attention and common knowledge: cf. Siposova and Carpenter (2019) for more. I shall leave application of these to divine–human relations for another time.

justification, moving toward externalist and socialized approaches, while taking up detailed questions about evidence and disagreement. More recent work also theorizes about other kinds of knowledge, including objectual or qualitative knowledge, practical knowledge, and even interpersonal knowledge. Such developments enable a richer set of resources for articulating a variety of ways in which one might bear epistemic relations to God, if there is a God, and for how to understand what faith in God can involve. The interpersonal epistemology adumbrated here takes seriously the possibility of knowledge about other persons, and the possibility of knowing them on relational terms. Developing such an interpersonal *religious* epistemology requires borrowing structural insights from the ways we know other humans, and the ways we love and put trust in other humans, and assuming that (by analogy) these insights are applicable to our relationship with a personal God.

References

Adams, Robert Merrihew. 1984. "The Virtue of Faith." *Faith and Philosophy* 1: 3–15.

Adams, Robert Merrihew. 1999. *Finite and Infinite Goods: A Framework for Ethics*. Oxford: Oxford University Press.

Allison, Dale C. 2022. *Encountering Mystery: Religious Experience in a Secular Age*. Grand Rapids: Eerdmans.

Alston, William P. 1982. "Religious Experience and Religious Belief." *Noûs* 16: 3–12.

Alston, William P. 1991. *Perceiving God: The Epistemology of Religious Experience*. Ithaca: Cornell University Press.

Anderson, Charity. 2018. "Hume, Defeat, and Miracle Reports." In Matthew A. Benton, John Hawthorne, and Dani Rabinowitz (eds.), *Knowledge, Belief, and God*, 13–28. Oxford: Oxford University Press.

Anscombe, G. E. M. 2008. *Faith in a Hard Ground: Essays in Religion, Philosophy, and Ethics*. Exeter: Imprint Academic.

Augustine. 1991. *The Trinity*. The Works of Saint Augustine. Hyde Park: New City Press.

Ayer, A.J. 1936. *Language, Truth, and Logic*. London: Gollancz.

Baillie, John. 1939. *Our Knowledge of God*. Oxford: Oxford University Press.

Baker, Mark and Zimmerman, Dean. 2019. "On Perceiving God: Prospects for a Cognitive Science of Religious Experience." In Alvin I. Goldman and Brian P. McLaughlin (eds.), *Metaphysics and Cognitive Science*, 125–154. New York: Oxford University Press.

Baker-Hytch, Max. 2018. "Testimony Amidst Diversity." In Matthew A. Benton, John Hawthorne, and Dani Rabinowitz (eds.), *Knowledge, Belief, and God: New Insights in Religious Epistemology*, 183–202. Oxford: Oxford University Press.

Baker-Hytch, Max and Benton, Matthew A. 2015. "Defeatism Defeated." *Philosophical Perspectives* 29: 40–66.

Benton, Matthew A. 2016. "Knowledge and Evidence You Should Have Had." *Episteme* 13: 471–479.

Benton, Matthew A. 2017. "Epistemology Personalized." *Philosophical Quarterly* 67: 813–834.

Benton, Matthew A. 2018a. "God and Interpersonal Knowledge." *Res Philosophica* 95: 421–447.

Benton, Matthew A. 2018b. "Pragmatic Encroachment and Theistic Knowledge." In Matthew A. Benton, John Hawthorne, and Dani Rabinowitz (eds.), *Knowledge, Belief, and God*, 267–287. Oxford: Oxford University Press.

Benton, Matthew A. 2021. "Disagreement and Religion." In Matthew A. Benton and Jonathan L. Kvanvig (eds.), *Religious Disagreement and Pluralism*, 1–40. Oxford: Oxford University Press.

Benton, Matthew A., Hawthorne, John, and Isaacs, Yoaav. 2016. "Evil and Evidence." *Oxford Studies in Philosophy of Religion* 7: 1–31.

Benton, Matthew A., Hawthorne, John, and Rabinowitz, Dani (eds.). 2018. *Knowledge, Belief, and God: New Insights in Religious Epistemology*. Oxford: Oxford University Press.

Benton, Matthew A. and Kvanvig, Jonathan L. (eds.). 2021. *Religious Disagreement and Pluralism*. Oxford: Oxford University Press.

Bergmann, Michael. 2006. *Justification without Awareness: A Defense of Epistemic Externalism*. Oxford: Oxford University Press.

Bergmann, Michael. 2017. "Foundationalism." In William J. Abraham and Frederick D. Aquino (eds.), *The Oxford Handbook of the Epistemology of Theology*, 253–273. Oxford: Oxford University Press.

Bogardus, Tomas and Urban, Mallorie. 2017. "How to Tell whether Christians and Muslims Worship the Same God." *Faith and Philosophy* 34: 176–200.

Brent, James. 2017. "Thomas Aquinas." In William J. Abraham and Frederick D. Aquino (eds.), *The Oxford Handbook of the Epistemology of Theology*, 408–420. Oxford: Oxford University Press.

Brooks, David. 2023. *How to Know a Person: The Art of Seeing Others Deeply and Being Deeply Seen*. New York: Random House.

Buber, Martin. 1937. *I and Thou*. Edinburgh: T&T Clark.

Buchak, Lara. 2012. "Can It Be Rational to Have Faith?" In Jake Chandler and Victoria S. Harrison (eds.), *Probability in the Philosophy of Religion*, 225–247. Oxford: Oxford University Press.

Buchak, Lara. 2014. "Reason and Faith." In William J. Abraham and Frederick D. Aquino (eds.), *The Oxford Handbook of the Epistemology of Theology*, 46–63. Oxford: Oxford University Press.

Burge, Tyler. 1977. "Belief *De Re*." *Journal of Philosophy* 74: 338–362.

Cockayne, Joshua. 2020. *Contemporary with Christ: Kierkegaard and Second-Personal Spirituality*. Waco: Baylor University Press.

Cook Wilson, John. 1926a. "Rational Grounds for Belief in God." In A. S. L. Farquharson (ed.), *Statement and Inference*, Volume 2, 835–865. Oxford: Clarendon Press.

Cook Wilson, John. 1926b. *Statement and Inference*, Volume 1. Oxford: Clarendon Press.

Craig, Edward. 1991. *Knowledge and the State of Nature: An Essay in Conceptual Synthesis.* Oxford: Clarendon Press.

Cullison, Andrew. 2010. "Two Solutions to the Problem of Divine Hiddenness." *American Philosophical Quarterly* 47: 119–134.

Cuneo, Terence. 2016. *Ritualized Faith: Essays on the Philosophy of Liturgy.* Oxford: Oxford University Press.

Dalmiya, Vrinda. 2016. *Caring to Know: Comparative Care Ethics, Feminist Epistemology, and the Mahābhārata.* New Delhi: Oxford University Press.

De Cruz, Helen. 2019. *Religious Disagreement.* Cambridge Elements in Philosophy of Religion. Cambridge: Cambridge University Press.

DeRose, Keith. 2018. "Delusions of Knowledge Concerning God's Existence." In Matthew A. Benton, John Hawthorne, and Dani Rabinowitz (eds.), *Knowledge, Belief, and God,* 288–301. Oxford: Oxford University Press.

Dietz, Christina and Hawthorne, John. 2023. "Knowledge-First Epistemology and Religious Belief." In Jonathan Fuqua, John Greco, and Tyler Dalton McNabb (eds.), *The Cambridge Handbook of Religious Epistemology,* forthcoming, 257–272. Cambridge: Cambridge University Press.

Dole, Andrew and Chignell, Andrew (eds.). 2005. *God and the Ethics of Belief: New Essays in Philosophy of Religion.* Cambridge: Cambridge University Press.

Dormandy, Katherine. 2021. "The Loyalty of Religious Disagremement." In Matthew A. Benton and Jonathan L. Kvanvig (eds.), *Religious Disagreement and Pluralism,* 238–270. Oxford: Oxford University Press.

Dunaway, Billy. 2020. *Reality and Morality.* Oxford: Oxford University Press.

Dunaway, Billy and Hawthorne, John. 2017. "Scepticism." In William J. Abraham and Frederick D. Aquino (eds.), *The Oxford Handbook of the Epistemology of Theology,* 290–308. Oxford: Oxford University Press.

Duncan, Matt. 2020. "Knowledge of Things." *Synthese* 197: 3559–3592.

Ellis, Fiona (ed.). 2018. *New Models of Religious Understanding.* Oxford: Oxford University Press.

Farkas, Katalin. 2016. "Know-Wh Does Not Reduce to Know That." *American Philosophical Quarterly* 53: 109–122.

Farkas, Katalin. 2019. "Objectual Knowledge." In Jonathan Knowles and Thomas Raleigh (eds.), *Acquaintance: New Essays,* 260–276. Oxford: Oxford University Press.

Flew, Antony. 1966. *God and Philosophy.* New York: Harcourt, Brace, and World.

Flew, Antony, Hare, R.M., and Mitchell, Basil. 1955. "Theology and Falsification." In Antony Flew and Alasdair MacIntyre (eds.), *New Essays in Philosophical Theology,* 96–108. London: SCM Press.

Fraser, Rachel. 2021. "Narrative Testimony." *Philosophical Studies* 178: 4025–4052.

Fraser, Rachel Elizabeth. 2018. "Testimonial Pessimism." In Matthew A. Benton, John Hawthorne, and Dani Rabinowitz (eds.), *Knowledge, Belief, and God*, 203–227. Oxford: Oxford University Press.

Fricker, Elizabeth. 1995. "Critical Notice: Telling and Trusting: Reductionism and Anti-Reductionism in the Epistemology of Testimony." *Mind* 104: 393–411.

Fricker, Miranda. 2007. *Epistemic Injustice: Power and the Ethics of Knowing*. Oxford: Oxford University Press.

Gettier, Edmund. 1963. "Is Justified True Belief Knowledge?" *Analysis* 23: 121–123.

Gladwell, Malcolm. 2019. *Talking to Strangers: What We Should Know about the People We Don't Know*. Boston: Little, Brown.

Goldberg, Sanford C. 2014. "Does Externalist Epistemology Rationalize Religious Commitment?" In Laura Frances Callahan and Timothy O'Connor (eds.), *Religious Faith and Intellectual Virtue*, 279–298. Oxford: Oxford University Press.

Goldberg, Sanford C. 2016. "On the Epistemic Significance of Evidence You Should Have Had." *Episteme* 13: 449–470.

Goldberg, Sanford C. 2021. "How Confident Should the Religious Believer Be in the Face of Religious Pluralism?" In Matthew A. Benton and Jonathan L. Kvanvig (eds.), *Religious Disagreement and Pluralism*, 65–90. Oxford: Oxford University Press.

Goldman, Alvin I. 1967. "A Causal Theory of Knowing." Reprinted in Goldman (1992).

Goldman, Alvin I. 1986. *Epistemology and Cognition*. Cambridge, MA: Harvard University Press.

Goldman, Alvin I. 1992. *Liaisons: Philosophy Meets the Cognitive and Social Sciences*. Cambridge, MA: The MIT Press.

Goldman, Alvin I. 2019. "God and Cognitive Science: A Bayesian Approach." In Alvin I. Goldman and Brian P. McLaughlin (eds.), *Metaphysics and Cognitive Science*, 155–179. New York: Oxford University Press.

Gómez, Juan Carlos. 1996. "Second Person Intentional Relations and the Evolution of Social Understanding." *Behavioral and Brain Sciences* 19: 129–130.

Gómez, Juan Carlos. 2005. "Joint Attention and the Notion of Subject." In Naomi Eilan, Christopher Hoerl, Teresa McCormack, and Johannes Roessler (eds.), *Joint Attention: Communication and Others Minds*, 65–84. Oxford: Clarendon Press.

Gómez, Juan Carlos. 2022. "Intentionality in the Second Person: An Evolutionary Perspective." *Teorema* 41: 49–64.

Greco, Daniel. 2015a. "Iteration and Fragmentation." *Philosophy and Phenomenological Research* 91: 656–673.

Greco, John. 2010. *Achieving Knowledge*. Cambridge: Cambridge University Press.

Greco, John. 2015b. "No-Fault Atheism." In Adam Green and Eleonore Stump (eds.), *Hidden Divinity and Religious Belief: New Perspectives*, 109–125. Cambridge: Cambridge University Press.

Greco, John. 2017. "Knowledge of God." In William J. Abraham and Frederick D. Aquino (eds.), *The Oxford Handbook of the Epistemology of Theology*, 9–29. Oxford: Oxford University Press.

Green, Adam. 2012. "Perceiving Persons." *Journal of Consciousness Studies* 19: 49–64.

Green, Adam. 2015. "Hiddenness and the Epistemology of Attachment." In Adam Green and Eleonore Stump (eds.), *Hidden Divinity and Religious Belief: New Perspectives*, 139–154. Cambridge: Cambridge University Press.

Green, Adam. 2021. "Forgiveness and the Repairing of Epistemic Trust." *Episteme* 1–21. https://doi.org/10.1017/epi.2021.27.

Griffioen, Amber L. 2022. "Rethinking Religious Epistemology." *European Journal for Philosophy of Religion* 14: 21–47. https://doi.org/10.24204/ejpr.2022.3290.

Hare, John E. 2007. *God and Morality: A Philosophical History*. Malden: Blackwell.

Hawthorne, John. 2004. *Knowledge and Lotteries*. Oxford: Clarendon Press.

Hawthorne, John and Isaacs, Yoaav. 2018. "Fine-Tuning Fine-Tuning." In Matthew A. Benton, John Hawthorne, and Dani Rabinowitz (eds.), *Knowledge, Belief, and God*, 136–168. Oxford: Oxford University Press.

Howard-Snyder, Daniel. 2013. "Propositional Faith: What It Is, and What It Is Not." *American Philosophical Quarterly* 50: 357–372.

Howard-Snyder, Daniel. 2017. "Markan Faith." *International Journal for Philosophy of Religion* 81: 31–60.

Howard-Snyder, Daniel and McKaughan, Daniel J. 2022. "Faith and Resilience." *International Journal for Philosophy of Religion* 91: 205–241.

Immerman, Daniel. 2022. "How Common Knowledge Is Possible." *Mind* 131: 935–948.

Jackson, Elizabeth. 2023. "Faith: Contemporary Perspectives." *Internet Encyclopedia of Philosophy*. https://iep.utm.edu/faith–contemporary–perspectives/.

Jackson, Frank. 1982. "Epiphenomenal Qualia." *Philosophical Quarterly* 32: 127–136.

Jackson, Frank. 1986. "What Mary Didn't Know." *Journal of Philosophy* 83: 291–295.

James, William. 1912. *The Will to Believe, and Other Essays in Popular Philosophy*. New York: Longmans, Green.

Keller, Lorraine Juliano. 2018. "Divine Ineffability and Franciscan Knowledge." *Res Philosophica* 95: 347–370.

Kelly, Thomas. 2011. "*Consensus Gentium*: Reflections on the 'Common Consent' Argument for the Existence of God." In Kelly James Clark and Raymond J. VanArragon (eds.), *Evidence and Religious Belief*, 135–156. Oxford: Oxford University Press.

Kelp, Christoph. 2023. *The Nature and Normativity of Defeat*. Cambridge: Cambridge University Press.

Kemp Smith, Norman. 1931. *Is Divine Existence Credible?* British Academy Lecture. London: Humphrey Milford.

Klein, Peter. 1971. "A Proposed Definition of Propositional Knowledge." *Journal of Philosophy* 68: 471–482.

Knight, John Allan. 2013. *Liberalism versus Postliberalism: The Great Divide in Twentieth-Century Theology*. Oxford: Oxford University Press.

Kolodny, Niko. 2003. "Love Is Valuing a Relationship." *Philosophical Review* 112: 135–189.

Kukla, Quill R. 2023. "Knowing Things and Going Places." *European Journal of Philosophy* 31: 266–282.

Kvanvig, Jonathan L. 2018. *Faith and Humility*. Oxford: Oxford University Press.

Lackey, Jennifer. 2008. *Learning from Words: Testimony as a Source of Knowledge*. Oxford: Oxford University Press.

Lasonen-Aarnio, Maria. 2010. "Unreasonable Knowledge." *Philosophical Perspectives* 24: 1–21.

Lasonen-Aarnio, Maria. 2014. "Higher-Order Evidence and the Limits of Defeat." *Philosophy and Phenomenological Research* 88: 314–345.

Lazerowitz, Morris. 1942. "Moore's Paradox." In Paul Arthur Schilpp (ed.), *The Philosophy of G.E. Moore*, The Library of Living Philosophers, 369–393. La Salle: Open Court Press.

Lebens, Samuel. 2013. "The Epistemology of Religiosity: An Orthodox Jewish Perspective." *International Journal for Philosophy of Religion* 74: 315–332.

Lebens, Samuel. 2023. "Amen to *daat*: On the Foundations of Jewish Epistemology." *Religious Studies* 59: 465–478.

Lederman, Harvey. 2017. "Uncommon Knowledge." *Mind* 127: 1069–1105.

Lewis, C. S. 1955. "On Obstinacy in Belief." *The Sewanee Review* 63: 525–538.

Lewis, C. S. 1959. "The Efficacy of Prayer." *The Atlantic Monthly* 203: 59–61.

Lindemann, Hilde. 2014. *Holding and Letting Go: The Social Practice of Personal Identities*. Oxford: Oxford University Press.

Luhrmann, T. M. 2012. *When God Talks Back: Understanding the American Evangelical Relationship with God*. New York: Vintage Books.

Luhrmann, T. M. 2020. *How God Becomes Real: Kindling the Presence of Invisible Others*. Princeton: Princeton University Press.

MacIntyre, Alasdair. 1988. *Whose Justice? Which Rationality?* Notre Dame: University of Notre Dame Press.

Marion, Mathieu. 2000. "Oxford Realism: Knowledge and Perception I." *British Journal for the History of Philosophy* 8: 299–338.

Martin, Adrienne M. 2019. "Interpersonal Hope." In Claudia Blöser and Titus Stahl (eds.), *The Moral Psychology of Hope*, 229–247. London: Rowman and Littlefield.

Mason, Cathy. 2020. "The Epistemic Demands of Friendship: Friendship as Inherently Knowledge-Involving." *Synthese* 199: 2439–2455.

McKaughan, Daniel J. 2017. "On the Value of Faith and Faithfulness." *International Journal for Philosophy of Religion* 81: 7–29.

McNabb, Tyler Dalton. 2019. *Religious Epistemology*. Cambridge Elements in Philosophy of Religion. Cambridge: Cambridge University Press.

Medina, José. 2013. *The Epistemology of Resistance: Gender and Racial Oppression, Epistemic Injustice, and Resistant Imaginations*. Oxford: Oxford University Press.

Mitchell, Basil (ed.). 1958. *Faith and Logic: Oxford Essays in Philosophical Theology*. London: George Allen & Unwin.

Moon, Andrew. 2016. "Recent Work in Reformed Epistemology." *Philosophy Compass* 11: 879–891.

Mooney, T. Brian and Williams, John N. 2017. "Valuable Asymmetrical Friendships." *Philosophy* 92: 51–76.

Moore, G. E. 1959. *Philosophical Papers*. London: George Allen & Unwin.

Morgan, Teresa. 2022. *The New Testament and the Theology of Trust: "This Rich Trust."* Oxford: Oxford University Press.

Moss, Jessica. forthcoming. "Knowledge-that is Knowledge-of." *Philosophers' Imprint* https://doi.org/10.3998/phimp.3339.

Murdoch, Iris. 2014 [1970]. *The Sovereignty of Good*. London: Routledge & Kegan Paul.

Nagel, Thomas. 1974. "What Is It Like to Be a Bat?" *The Philosophical Review* 83: 435–450.

Oppy, Graham. 2006. *Arguing about Gods*. Cambridge: Cambridge University Press.

Page, Ben. 2019. "Wherein Lies the Debate? Concerning whether God Is a Person." *International Journal for Philosophy of Religion* 85: 297–317.

Pettigrove, Glen. 2012. *Forgiveness and Love*. Oxford: Oxford University Press.

Pittard, John. 2020. *Disagreement, Deference, and Religious Commitment*. Oxford: Oxford University Press.

Plantinga, Alvin. 1967. *God and Other Minds: A Study of the Rational Justification of Belief in God*. Ithaca: Cornell University Press.

Plantinga, Alvin. 1993. *Warrant and Proper Function*. New York: Oxford University Press.

Plantinga, Alvin. 2000. *Warranted Christian Belief*. New York: Oxford University Press.

Plantinga, Alvin and Wolterstorff, Nicholas (eds.). 1983. *Faith and Rationality: Reason and Belief in God*. Notre Dame: University of Notre Dame Press.

Pollock, John L. 1986. *Contemporary Theories of Knowledge*. Totowa: Rowman & Littlefield, 1st ed. 2nd ed.: 1999, with Joseph Cruz.

Price, H. H. 1965. "Belief 'In' and Belief 'That'." *Religious Studies* 1: 5–27.

Prichard, H. A. 1909. *Kant's Theory of Knowledge*. Oxford: Oxford University Press.

Pritchard, Duncan. 2000. "Is 'God Exists' a 'Hinge Proposition' of Religious Belief?" *International Journal for Philosophy of Religion* 47: 129–140.

Pritchard, Duncan. 2012. "Wittgenstein and the Groundlessness of Our Believing." *Synthese* 189: 255–272.

Rawls, John. 2009. *A Brief Inquiry into the Meaning of Sin and Faith: With "On My Religion."* Cambridge, MA: Harvard University Press.

Rea, Michael C. 2018. *The Hiddenness of God*. Oxford: Oxford University Press.

Reddy, Vasudevi. 2008. *How Infants Know Minds*. Cambridge, MA: Harvard University Press.

Ritchie, Sarah Lane. 2021. "Integrated Physicality and the Absence of God: Spiritual Technologies in Theological Context." *Modern Theology* 37: 296–315.

Russell, Bertrand. 1910. "Knowledge by Acquaintance and Knowledge by Description." *Proceedings of the Aristotelian Society* 11: 108–128.

Russell, Bertrand. 1998 [1912]. *The Problems of Philosophy*. Oxford: Oxford University Press, 2nd ed.

Ryle, Gilbert. 1949. *The Concept of Mind*. London: Hutchinson.

Saunders, Leland F. 2021. "Virtues as Reasons Structures." *Philosophical Studies* 178: 2785–2804.

Schellenberg, J. L. 2008. "What Divine Hiddenness Reveals." https://infidels .org/library/modern/john_schellenberg/hidden.html.

Schellenberg, J. L. 1993. *Divine Hiddenness and Human Reason*. Ithaca: Cornell University Press.

Schellenberg, J. L. 2015a. "Divine Hiddenness and Human Philosophy." In Adam Green and Eleonore Stump (eds.), *Hidden Divinity and Religious Belief: New Perspectives*, 13–32. Cambridge: Cambridge University Press.

Schellenberg, J. L. 2015b. *The Hiddenness Argument*. Oxford: Oxford University Press.

Scotus, John Duns. 1997. *Questions on the Metaphysics of Aristotle*, Volume 2, Books 6–9. St. Bonaventure: Franciscan Institute.

Setiya, Kieran. 2023. "Other People." In Sarah Buss and Nandi Theunissen (eds.), *Rethinking the Value of Humanity*, 314–336. Oxford: Oxford University Press.

Siegel, Daniel J. 2020. *The Developing Mind: How Relationships and the Brain Interact to Shape Who We Are*. New York: The Guilford Press.

Simpson, Thomas W. 2023. *Trust: A Philosophical Study*. Oxford: Oxford University Press.

Siposova, Barbora and Carpenter, Malinda. 2019. "A New Look at Joint Attention and Common Knowledge." *Cognition* 189: 260–274.

Sliwa, Paulina. 2018. "Know-How and Acts of Faith." In Matthew A. Benton, John Hawthorne, and Dani Rabinowitz (eds.), *Knowledge, Belief, and God*, 246–263. Oxford: Oxford University Press.

Sosa, Ernest. 1999. "How to Defeat Opposition to Moore." *Philosophical Perspectives* 13: 142–153.

Sosa, Ernest. 2006. "Knowledge: Instrumental and Testimonial." In Jennifer Lackey and Ernest Sosa (eds.), *The Epistemology of Testimony*, 116–123. Oxford: Oxford University Press.

Sosa, Ernest. 2007. *A Virtue Epistemology: Apt Belief and Reflective Knowledge*, Volume 1. Oxford: Clarendon Press.

Sosa, Ernest. 2009. *Reflective Knowledge: Apt Belief and Reflective Knowledge*, Volume 2. Oxford: Clarendon Press.

Sosa, Ernest. 2011. *Knowing Full Well*. Princeton: Princeton University Press.

Sosa, Ernest. 2015. *Judgment and Agency*. Oxford: Oxford University Press.

Sosa, Ernest. 2021. *Epistemic Explanations: A Theory of Epistemic Normativity, and What It Explains*. Oxford: Oxford University Press.

Srinivasan, Amia. 2020. "Radical Externalism." *The Philosophical Review* 129: 395–431.

Stanley, Jason. 2011. *Know How*. Oxford: Oxford University Press.

Stanley, Jason and Williamson, Timothy. 2001. "Knowing How." *Journal of Philosophy* 98: 411–444.

Strabbing, Jada Twedt. 2017. "Divine Forgiveness and Reconciliation." *Faith and Philosophy* 34: 272–297.

Stump, Eleonore. 2010. *Wandering in Darkness: Narrative and the Problem of Suffering*. Oxford: Clarendon Press.

Stump, Eleonore. 2011. "Eternity, Simplicity, and Presence." In Gregory T. Doolan (ed.), *The Science of Being as Being: Metaphysical Investigations*, 243–263. Washington, DC: Catholic University of America Press.

Stump, Eleonore. 2017. "Theology and the Knowledge of Persons." In Fiona Ellis (ed.), *New Models of Religious Understanding*, 172–190. Oxford: Oxford University Press.

Sullivan, Meghan. 2012. "Semantics of Blasphemy." *Oxford Studies in Philosophy of Religion* 4: 159–173.

Sullivan, Meghan. 2015. "The Semantic Problem of Hiddenness." In Adam Green and Eleonore Stump (eds.), *Hidden Divinity and Religious Belief*, 35–52. Cambridge: Cambridge University Press.

Swanton, Christine. 2003. *Virtue Ethics: A Pluralistic View*. Oxford: Oxford University Press.

Swinburne, Richard. 2001. *Epistemic Justification*. Oxford: Clarendon Press.

Swinburne, Richard. 2004. *The Existence of God*. Oxford: Oxford University Press, 2nd ed.

Swinburne, Richard. 2005. *Faith and Reason*. Oxford: Clarendon Press, 2nd ed.

Talbert, Bonnie M. 2015. "Knowing Other People: A Second-Person Framework." *Ratio* 28: 190–206.

Taliaferro, Charles. 2017. "Love and Philosophy of Religion: Lessons from the Cambridge Platonists." In Fiona Ellis (ed.), *New Models of Religious Understanding*, 208–226. Oxford: Oxford University Press.

Um, Sungwoo. 2021. "What Is a Relational Virtue?" *Philosophical Studies* 178: 95–111.

Wainwright, William J. 2002. "Jonathan Edwards and the Hiddenness of God." In Daniel Howard-Snyder and Paul K. Moser (eds.), *Divine Hiddenness: New Essays*, 98–119. Cambridge: Cambridge University Press.

Warmke, Brandon. 2016. "The Normative Significance of Forgiveness." *Australasian Journal of Philosophy* 94: 687–703.

Warmke, Brandon. 2017. "God's Standing to Forgive." *Faith and Philosophy* 34: 381–402.

Webb, Clement C. J. 1911. *Problems in the Relation of God and Man*. London: Nisbet.

Webb, Clement C. J. 1920. *Divine Personality and Human Life*. Gifford Lectures (1918–1919), 2nd course. London: George Allen & Unwin.

Wesley, John. 1988. *The Works of John Wesley*, Volume 18: Journals and Diaries I (1735–1738). Nashville: Abingdon Press.

Williamson, Timothy. 2000. *Knowledge and Its Limits*. Oxford: Oxford University Press.

Williamson, Timothy. 2014. "Very Improbable Knowing." *Erkenntnis* 79: 971–999.

Wisdom, John. 1945. "Gods." *Proceedings of the Aristotelian Society* 45: 185–206.

Wittgenstein, Ludwig. 1969. *On Certainty*. Oxford: Blackwell.

Wolterstorff, Nicholas P. 1995. *Divine Discourse: Philosophical Reflections on the Claim that God Speaks*. Cambridge: Cambridge University Press.

Wolterstorff, Nicholas P. 2016. "Knowing God Liturgically." *Journal of Analytic Theology* 4: 1–16.

Wolterstorff, Nicholas P. 2021. "Knowing God by Liturgically Addressing God." In Joshua Cockayne and Jonathan C. Rutledge (eds.), *United in Love: Essays on Justice, Art, and Liturgy*, 214–239. Eugene: Cascade Books.

Zagzebski, Linda Trinkaus. 2012. *Epistemic Authority: A Theory of Trust, Authority, and Autonomy in Belief*. Oxford: Oxford University Press.

Acknowledgments

This Element would not have been possible without the help and support of many others.

I am most thankful to Laura Benton, for the numerous ways she supports me in my work, and in all other things.

For helpful conversations or comments on some of these ideas, going back many years, I am grateful to Charity Anderson, Robert Audi, Alex Arnold, Max Baker-Hytch, Lara Buchak, Laura Callahan, Andrew Chignell, Isaac Choi, Joshua Cockayne, Troy Cross, Frank Curry, Keith DeRose, Billy Dunaway, David Efird, Lizzie Fricker, Peter Graham, Adam Green, Eric Gregory, Brian Hedden, Dan Howard-Snyder, Hud Hudson, Liz Jackson, Yoaav Isaacs, Tim Isaacson, Chris Kelp, Tim Mawson, Conor Mayo-Wilson, Patrick McDonald, Katie O'Dell, Glen Pettigrove, Dani Rabinowitz, Michael Rea, Rebekah Rice, Blake Roeber, Daniel Rubio, Jeff Sanford Russell, Leland Saunders, Meg Scharle, Mona Simion, Tom Simpson, Jason Stigall, Andrew Torrance, Chris Tucker, Nathaniel Warne, Nick Wolterstorff, David Worsley, Dean Zimmerman, and especially, to John Hawthorne, Timothy Williamson, and Ernie Sosa.

These ideas were also improved by audiences at presentations over many years, particularly those given at the University of Innsbruck, the University of York, Baylor University, the University of Missouri–St. Louis, Reed College, the University of Notre Dame, Princeton University, the University of St. Andrews, the University of Glasgow, and the University of Oxford. I am also thankful to my students who often read versions of this material for class, and provided illuminating discussion.

Finally, thanks to Stephen Hetherington, editor of the Elements in Epistemology series, and to two anonymous referees, for helpful feedback.

This Element was made possible through the support of a grant from the John Templeton Foundation (both as a fellow in the New Insights and Directions for Religious Epistemology project at Oxford, 2012–2015, and through a recent smaller grant on Knowledge and God). The opinions expressed in this publication are those of the author and do not necessarily reflect the views of the John Templeton Foundation.

Cambridge Elements

Epistemology

Stephen Hetherington
University of New South Wales, Sydney

Stephen Hetherington is Professor Emeritus of Philosophy at the University of New South Wales, Sydney. He is the author of numerous books, including *Knowledge and the Gettier Problem* (Cambridge University Press, 2016) and *What Is Epistemology?* (Polity, 2019), and is the editor of several others, including *Knowledge in Contemporary Epistemology* (with Markos Valaris: Bloomsbury, 2019) and *What the Ancients Offer to Contemporary Epistemology* (with Nicholas D. Smith: Routledge, 2020). He was the Editor-in-Chief of the Australasian Journal of Philosophy from 2013 until 2022.

About the Series

This Elements series seeks to cover all aspects of a rapidly evolving field, including emerging and evolving topics such as: fallibilism; knowinghow; self-knowledge; knowledge of morality; knowledge and injustice; formal epistemology; knowledge and religion; scientific knowledge; collective epistemology; applied epistemology; virtue epistemology; wisdom. The series demonstrates the liveliness and diversity of the field, while also pointing to new areas of investigation

Cambridge Elements ≡

Epistemology

Printed in the United States
by Baker & Taylor Publisher Services